Did you all know? If you eat stuff like squid-ink spaghetti, your poop turns black. Pitch black. Hey, so what do you think? If you eat rainbow-colored spaghetti, do you think your poop will be rainbow-colored? I wonder. Maybe it doesn't matter.

-Eiichiro Oda, 1998

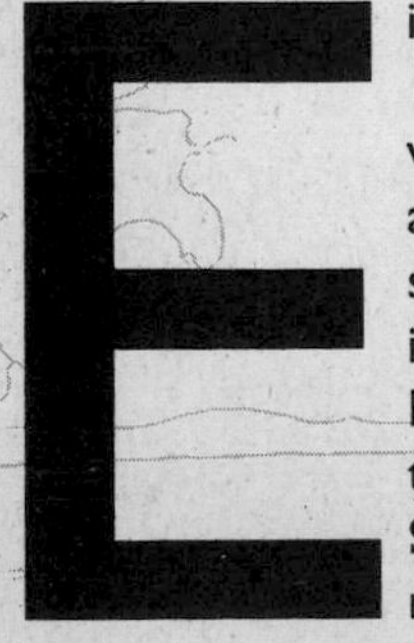

Eiichiro Oda began his manga career at the age of 17, when his one-shot cowboy manga **Wanted!** won second place in the coveted Tezuka manga awards. Oda went on to work as an assistant to some of the biggest manga artists in the industry, including Nobuhiro Watsuki, before winning the Hop Step Award for new artists. His pirate adventure **One Piece**, which debuted in **Weekly Shonen Jump** in 1997, quickly became one of the most popular manga in Japan.

ONE PIECE VOL. 6
The SHONEN JUMP Manga Edition

This manga contains material that was originally published in English in **SHONEN JUMP** #23-25.

STORY AND ART BY EIICHIRO ODA

English Adaptation/Lance Caselman
Translation/Naoko Amemiya
Touch-up Art & Lettering/Mark McMurray
Design/Sean Lee
Editor/Megan Bates

Editor in Chief, Books/Alvin Lu
Editor in Chief, Magazines/Marc Weidenbaum
VP of Publishing Licensing/Rika Inouye
VP of Sales/Gonzalo Ferreyra
Sr. VP of Marketing/Liza Coppola
Publisher/Hyoe Narita

Printed in the U.S.A.

Published by VIZ Media, LLC
P.O. Box 77010
San Francisco, CA 94107

SHONEN JUMP Manga Edition
10 9 8 7 6 5
First printing, February 2005
Fifth printing, April 2008

www.viz.com

PARENTAL ADVISORY
ONE PIECE is rated T for Teen and is recommended for ages 13 and up. This volume contains fantasy violence and alcohol and tobacco usage.

ratings.viz.com

www.shonenjump.com

SHONEN JUMP MANGA

ONE PIECE

Vol. 6

THE OATH

STORY AND ART BY **EIICHIRO ODA**

Monkey D. Luffy
Gifted with rubber powers and bottomless optimism, he's determined to become King of the Pirates.

Roronoa Zolo
A former bounty hunter and master of the "three-sword" fighting style (one in each hand and one in his mouth!).

Usopp
The newest addition to Luffy's crew, Usopp's known for his tall tales, but he has a way with a slingshot and a heart of gold.

Nami
A thief who specializes in robbing pirates. Although she hates pirates, Luffy has convinced her to join his crew as navigator.

THE STORY OF ONE PIECE

Volume 6

Monkey D. Luffy started out as just a kid with a dream – and that dream was to become the greatest pirate in history! Stirred by the tales of pirate "Red-Haired" Shanks, Luffy vowed to become a pirate himself. That was before the enchanted Devil Fruit gave Luffy the power to stretch like rubber, at the cost of being unable to swim – a serious handicap for an aspiring sea dog. Undeterred, Luffy set out to sea and recruited some crewmates: lying sharpshooter Usopp, master swordsman Zolo and treasure-hunting thief Nami.

After stopping at a seaside village in search of food and a sturdy ship, Luffy and his crew meet Usopp, a boy who is famous as the town liar. When Usopp happens upon a dastardly plot to kill local girl Kaya, Luffy and his crew step into an intense battle against ruthless Captain Kuro and his Black Cat pirates. With Usopp's help, Kuro is defeated and Luffy's crew gains not only new crewmember Usopp but also a new ship, the Merry Go.

Luffy's next quest? To find a ship's cook, of course. Zolo's old bounty-hunting pals, Yosaku and Johnny, tell Luffy and crew about the oceangoing restaurant Baratie. Unfortunately, Luffy accidentally ricochets a cannonball into the floating food emporium, and to recompense he ends up working as Baratie's chore-boy. There he meets sous-chef Sanji, who will feed any pirate in need and would make a perfect ship's cook for the Merry Go...if only he wanted to jump ship!

Sanji
The sous-chef and maitre d' on the oceangoing restaurant Baratie. He has a keen sense of taste and likes the ladies.

Chef Zeff
A peg-legged pirate who runs the Baratie.

Hawk Eye Mihawk
Mysterious swordsman.

Don Krieg
Commander of the Pirate Armada.

"Red-Haired" Shanks
A pirate captain who saved young Luffy's life and inspired him with a love of the sea.

Yosaku and Johnny
Dim-witted bounty hunter brothers—they know Zolo from another life.

Vol. 6
THE OATH

CONTENTS

Chapter 45:
BEFORE THE STORM

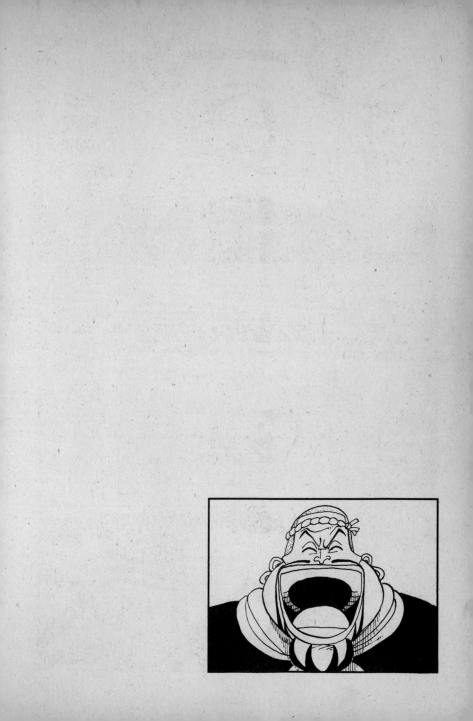

DO—M
YOU SURE GOT LUCKY!!
THAT FOOD SAVED YOU!!

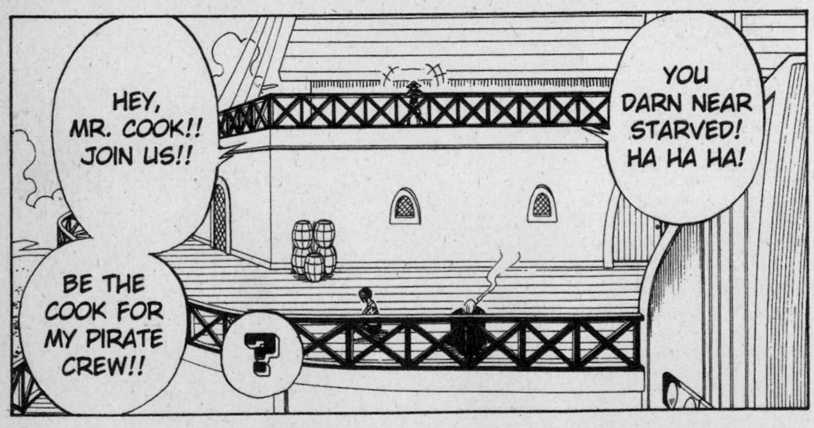
YOU DARN NEAR STARVED! HA HA HA!
HEY, MR. COOK!! JOIN US!!
BE THE COOK FOR MY PIRATE CREW!!
?

HUH?!!

YOU'RE...
...A PIRATE?!
WHY DID YOU FIRE ON US?
IT WAS AN ACCIDENT. A STRAY CANNON-BALL LAUNCHED IN SELF-DEFENSE.
THAT MAKES NO SENSE.

WELL, YOU'D BEST WATCH YOUR-SELF AROUND HERE.
CHEF ZEFF USED TO COOK FOR A FAMOUS PIRATE.
THAT OLD MAN WAS A PIRATE?
BARATIE IS THE OLD RATBAG'S TREASURE.

AND THE COOKS WHO FLOCK TO HIM ARE ALL HOT-BLOODED PIRATE TYPES.
FOR A PLACE FREQUENTED BY PIRATES, THEY'RE PERFECT FOR THE JOB.

READ THIS WAY

YEAH, THIS PLACE IS A NUTHOUSE.
ONE GROWS USED TO IT.
SOME PEOPLE COME JUST TO SEE THE PIRATES AND THE COOKS GO AT IT.

BUT THE WAITERS GOT SCARED...
...AND JUMPED SHIP.

OH...SO THAT'S WHY HE WANTS ME TO WORK FOR A YEAR.
ANYWAY, YOU SHOULD SAIL WITH ME.

I DECLINE.
I'VE GOT A GOOD REASON FOR STAYING HERE.

NO!!!
DA-DO-O-M!!
I DECLINE!!!

WHAT?
DECLINE WHAT?
I DECLINE YOUR... DECLINATION!!
YOU'RE A GOOD COOK, AND YOU'RE JOINING MY CREW!!

NOW, HOLD ON... LISTEN TO MY REASON.
WHAT IS IT, THEN?

NONE OF YOUR BUSINESS.
YOU JUST TOLD ME TO LISTEN!!
......

I MEAN, RESPECT MY WISHES!! I'LL MAKE A FILLET OUTTA YOU, YOU CRAP-HAT KID!!
YOU MAKE FUN OF THIS HAT AND I'LL SEND YOU FLYING!!

READ THIS WAY

SORRY TO BUTT IN, BUT...
WHAT?!!
GRRR

I'M GIN, ONE OF KRIEG'S PIRATES.
IF YOU'RE REALLY A PIRATE, WHAT'S YOUR PRIZE?
PIRATE-AT-ARMS
Krieg's Crew

I'M AFTER THE ONE PIECE!
I'M GOING TO THE GRAND LINE!!

!
......

IF YOU DON'T HAVE A COOK, YOU MUST NOT HAVE MUCH OF A CREW YET.
THIS GUY MAKES FIVE!
DON'T COUNT ME!!
YOU DON'T SEEM LIKE A BAD SORT, SO I'LL GIVE YOU A WORD OF WARNING.

WHATEVER YOU DO...
...DON'T GO TO THE GRAND LINE.

YOU'RE YOUNG. DON'T RUSH TO YOUR DOOM.
THE SEAS ARE VAST. THE GRAND LINE IS JUST ONE NARROW ROUTE.
THERE ARE PLENTY OF SAFER WATERS TO PLUNDER.

HMM... REALLY?
DO YOU KNOW A LOT ABOUT THE GRAND LINE?

NOT MUCH... HARDLY ANYTHING AT ALL.
BUT ENOUGH SO IT SCARES ME!!

YOU'RE RATHER CHICKEN FOR ONE OF KRIEG'S MEN.
WHO'S KRIEG?

READ THIS WAY

BARATIE -- THE GALLEY
HORS D'OEUVRES FOR TABLE THREE!!
FWERRR
TAK TAK TAK
SERVE IT YOURSELF! WE GOT NO WAITERS!
KLANK KLANK!
KLANK!

MAKING TROUBLE FOR US, PATTY?
WHAT?
fwup
fwup

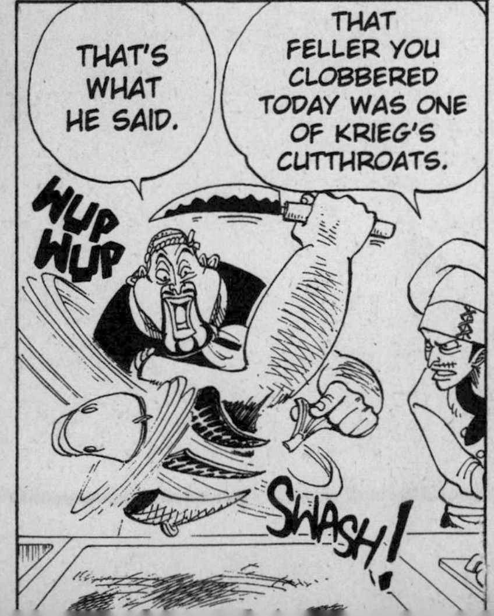

THAT FELLER YOU CLOBBERED TODAY WAS ONE OF KRIEG'S CUTTHROATS.
THAT'S WHAT HE SAID.
WUP WUP
SWASH!

DON KRIEG'S THE MEANEST PIRATE IN THESE HERE WATERS.

AYE...
HE'S DON OF THE PIRATE ARMADA-- A CONSORTIUM OF 50 PIRATE CREWS.
HE'S A PURE DEVIL!!

SO WHAT?!
OSH!
FWO
tptptptp...!!
HE COMMANDS 5,000 KILLERS! AND THAT FELLER WAS ONE OF 'EM!

IF HE TELLS DON KRIEG HOW HE WAS MISTREATED HERE, THEY'LL RUN OVER US LIKE...
...STAMPEDING ELEPHANTS!
THEY'LL MAKE MINCEMEAT OF US!

READ THIS WAY

WELL...

JUST THOUGHT I'D WARN YOU.
I'M GOING TO THE GRAND LINE ANYWAY.
HA HA... DO WHAT YOU WANT. HOW YOU THROW YOUR LIFE AWAY IS YOUR BUSINESS.

SANJI...
MY THANKS. YOU SAVED MY LIFE.
THAT GRUB WAS FINE.

CAN I COME AND EAT AGAIN?

ANY TIME.

CHORE BOY!! THERE YOU ARE!!
YIKES!! THE CHEF!!
....

KR
WHAT?
!?

YOU'RE GONNA CATCH HECK NOW...
...FOR GIVING ME A FREE MEAL.

......
GOOD LUCK, GIN.

SPLOOSH...!
FREE MEAL?
WHERE'S THE PROOF?

SANJI!! CHORE BOY!! GET TO WORK!!!

STAY OUT OF TROUBLE, GIN!!

FWERRRRRR
TAKTAKTAK!
KLANG
I'M LUFFY! BUT FOR NOW I'M...
CHORE BOY!!
REPORTING FOR DUTY!!
WHERE'S TABLE SIX'S DESSERT ?!
WHO TOOK THAT ORDER?
YOU DID, FOOL!
I'M TOO BUSY!
OPEN YOUR EYES!
YOU LOOKIN' FOR A FIGHT?
KLONK
krek...
IF YOU GOT NOTHING TO DO, WASH DISHES, CHORE BOY!!
OKEE-DOKE!
On Hiatus from Piracy
Free-Labor Chore Boy
MONKEY D. LUFFY

FLIRTING, OF COURSE.
AGAIN?!
AND HE'S *ASSISTANT CHEF*?! MAKES ME WANNA PUKE!!
FRRR
I KNOW, BUT HE'S BEEN HERE THE LONGEST.
FW
SHIK
EVER WONDER WHY SANJI STAYS, EVEN THOUGH HE DON'T GET ON WITH CHEF?

I'LL JUST CLEAN THIS WOK.
ksss

YOW!! H-HOT!!!
KRASH!!!
KLANG
KLANK
GET OUT OF THIS KITCHEN !!!
ploosh
ploosh

GO TAKE ORDERS!
JUST ASK THE CUSTOMERS WHAT THEY WANT TO EAT! THINK YOU CAN DO THAT?
nod
YESH.
SKRERK

AND TREAT THE CUSTOMERS LIKE I TOLD YOU!!
GOT IT.
PERFECT!

CHORES ARE HARD.
KOBY MUST HAVE BEEN MISER-ABLE.

HEY !!

DOOM!

CAN WE CHANGE THE SHIP'S FLAG?

blab blab

SO... YOU GOTTA WORK FOR A YEAR.

yack yack

HI, CHORE BOY.

UGH!! YOU GUYS?

GLUG GLUG
YOU DRINK IT!!
NO! GACK!!
ULP!
WHAT'D YOU DO THAT FOR?!
WHAT DID *YOU* DO THAT FOR?!
MY SIDES HURT!
wap wap wap
YECK

O SEA, HOW GRATEFUL I AM FOR THIS DAY OF DAYS!
O LOVE! ♥ SMILE UPON ME, FOR I CANNOT SURVIVE THIS PAIN.
D♥♥M!
I WOULD STOOP TO BECOMING A PIRATE, OR EVEN A DEVIL, IF ONLY I COULD BE WITH YOU. ♥
SUCH TRAGEDY!! THE OBSTACLES BETWEEN US ARE GREAT!!
?

OBSTACLES, SANJI?
ARGH! THE CRAP-GEEZER!!
FOLLOW YOUR HEART. GO BE A PIRATE.
I DON'T NEED YOU HERE ANYMORE.
DOOM!
WHAT?!

THAT'S HOW YOU MADE IT BACK, EH, GIN?
SO THIS COOK SAVED YOU FROM CERTAIN DEATH.
HMM...

WHAT?
...DON KRIEG.

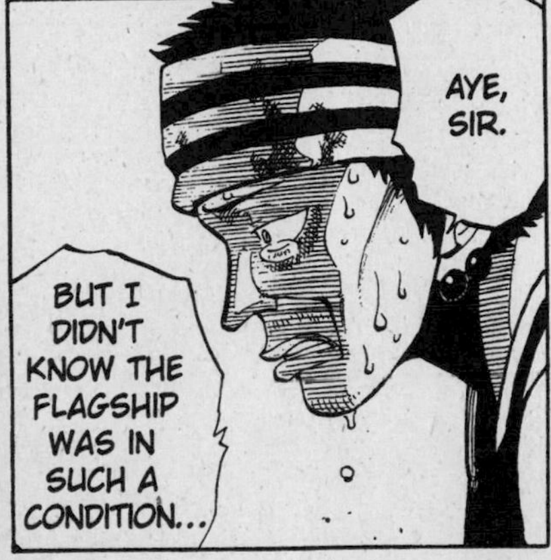
AYE, SIR.
BUT I DIDN'T KNOW THE FLAGSHIP WAS IN SUCH A CONDITION...

I'LL GUIDE YOU THERE.
TO BARATIE OCEANGOING RESTAURANT!

Q: Oda Sensei! One… two… Django!!!

A: Zzzzzzzzz… Huh? G'mornin'!!

Q: The other day, some neighborhood kids asked me, "Where can I go to meet Luffy?" So where can you go to meet Luffy? The North Sea? The Mediterranean? Tone River? Biwa Lake?

A: Hmm… where to go to meet him. That's difficult. If you were to take an unhurried journey around the world's oceans, you just might see him. But at sea you'll also encounter the likes of Buggy, so make sure you're careful. Always be careful.

Q: Umm, I have a question about "One-Two" Django. What's with the striped goatee?

A: It's a mushroom. Before becoming a pirate, he was a wandering dancer, but business was not good and he was always going to sleep without a bath. Then a striped mushroom started sprouting from his chin. He was hungry, so he ate the cap of the mushroom, but it tasted terrible! He swallowed it nonetheless, and ever since then he's been able to hypnotize people. So the stripes on his chin are actually the leftover bit of mushroom. Yup.

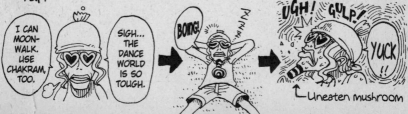

I CAN MOONWALK. USE CHAKRAM, TOO.
SIGH… THE DANCE WORLD IS SO TOUGH.
BOING!
UGH! GULP!
YUCK!!
Uneaten mushroom

Chapter 46:
AN UNINVITED GUEST

BUGGY'S CREW: AFTER THE BATTLE!
PART EIGHT: "DECISIVE DUEL IN THE FOREST"

HEY, CRAP-GEEZER.

I'M THE ASSISTANT CHEF HERE.
WHAT DO YOU MEAN, I'M NOT NEEDED?!

YOU FIGHT WITH THE CUSTOMERS.
YOU WASTE HOURS FLARING YOUR NOSTRILS FOR THE WOMEN.

AND YOU'RE A LOUSY COOK.
YOU'RE NOTHING BUT DEAD WEIGHT, SANJI.
THE OTHER COOKS DON'T MUCH LIKE YOU, EITHER.
SO GO BE A PIRATE AND GET OUT OF MY RESTAURANT.

DON'T STEP OVER THE LINE, OLD MAN!!!
WAP!!
YOU CAN INSULT ME, BUT DON'T EVER INSULT MY COOKING!!
......
I'M STAYING RIGHT HERE! YOU HAVE NO SAY IN THE MATTER!!!

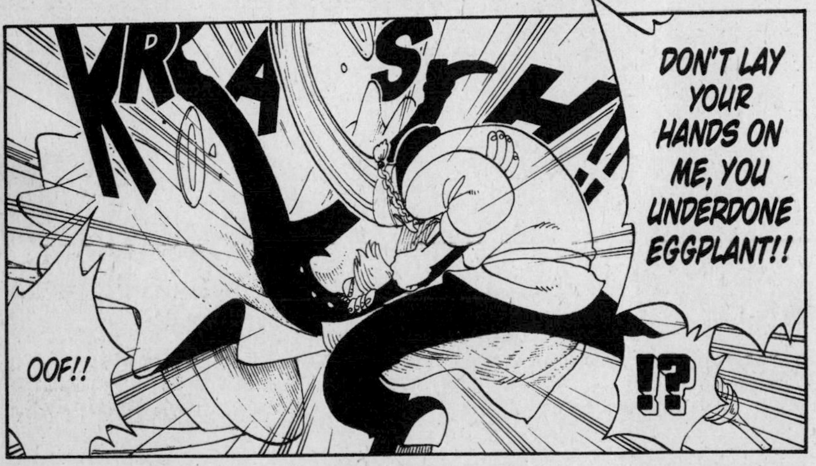
DON'T LAY YOUR HANDS ON ME, YOU UNDERDONE EGGPLANT!!
KRASH!!
!?
OOF!!

HMPH.

OUCH...

YOU CAN'T KICK ME OUT!!!
I'LL COOK HERE FOREVER!!!

DOOM
FORGIVE THE COMMOTION. A FRUIT *MACÉDOINE*, WITH MY COMPLIMENTS.
AND GRAND MARNIER AS A DIGESTIVE, MY PRINCESS.
OOOH, THANK YOU.
glup glup...

HOW GALLANT. ♡
NOT AT ALL...♡
HEY!
WAP!!
hee

DON'T *WE* GET ANY?!
THAT'S DISCRIMINATION! I'LL SUE!!
WAP
WAP
slurp slurp

I GAVE YOU TEA, DIDN'T I? YOU SHOULD BE GRATEFUL, YOU MANGY OCTOPUS!!
YOU WANNA FIGHT? I'M NOT GONNA TAKE THAT FROM YOU!! GET HIM, ZOLO!!
GET HIM YOURSELF.
......!
MMM, DELICIOUS.
FWIP

YOU HAVEN'T EVEN CLEARED MY PLATE!
THERE ARE MUSHROOMS ON IT. EAT THEM!!

I DON'T LIKE MUSHROOMS! I ATE A POISON MUSHROOM ONCE WHEN I WAS A KID!
WELL *THOSE* AREN'T POISONOUS, SO EAT EVERY BITE, LONG NOSE!!

OH, PLEASE DON'T FIGHT OVER ME!
gasp
AS YOU WISH. ♡
WHO'S FIGHTING OVER YOU?!

UM, CHEF DEAR?
swff
YES, MY SWEET? ♡
THIS GOURMET FARE IS A TAD PRICEY.

FOR YOU, IT'S FREE!! ♡
SKWSH!
HOORAY!! MY HERO!!
AHHH... ♡

PAY UP, YOU BUMS!!
WHAT?!!
SNORT!

DID YOU BEWITCH HIM?!
MM, GOOD TEA.
SUP SUP
AHH... LOVELY...
YOU THREE BETTER WATCH OUT, TOO.
hyuk

HI, SANJI! I'VE MISSED YOU!
SO NICE TO SEE YOU, ROXANNE!
I WANT MY FRUIT!
WHAT A LADY'S MAN.

ENOUGH GOOFING OFF, CHORE BOY!!
WOMP!!
SPLASH

OFFER HOT TOWELS TO OUR CUSTOMERS.
OKAY...
skff skff...

TWO DAYS LATER...
RESTAURANT
BARATIE
FROM OUT OF NOWHERE...

KREESH!!

DON KRIEG'S PIRATE SHIP!!!
FWAP
FWAP

GASP...
THE HOUR-GLASSES BESIDE THE SKULL MEAN THAT TIME'S RUN OUT FOR THEIR ENEMIES...

WOOOOO
THERE'S NO MISTAKE!! IT'S KRIEG'S PIRATES!!!
WHAT DO THEY WANT?!!
gasp
gasp
gasp

SEE, PATTY?! THEY'RE HERE! YOU DEAL WITH THEM!!!
IT C-C-CAN'T BE! THE DON OF THE PIRATE ARMADA AND HIS 5,000 MEN?! HERE?!!
WOULD THEY COME JUST TO AVENGE ONE FLUNKY?
WELL, THEY'RE HERE! THAT'S DEFINITELY HIS SHIP!!!

WHOA!! THIS IS BAD! LET'S GET OUTTA HERE!!!
klip klop
klip klop
BROTHER... SET SAIL! WE DON'T WANNA DIE!!!

THAT SHIP IS HUGE!! MAYBE GIN'S COME BACK TO SAY THANKS.
I DOUBT IT... BUT SOME-THING SEEMS ODD.

........?

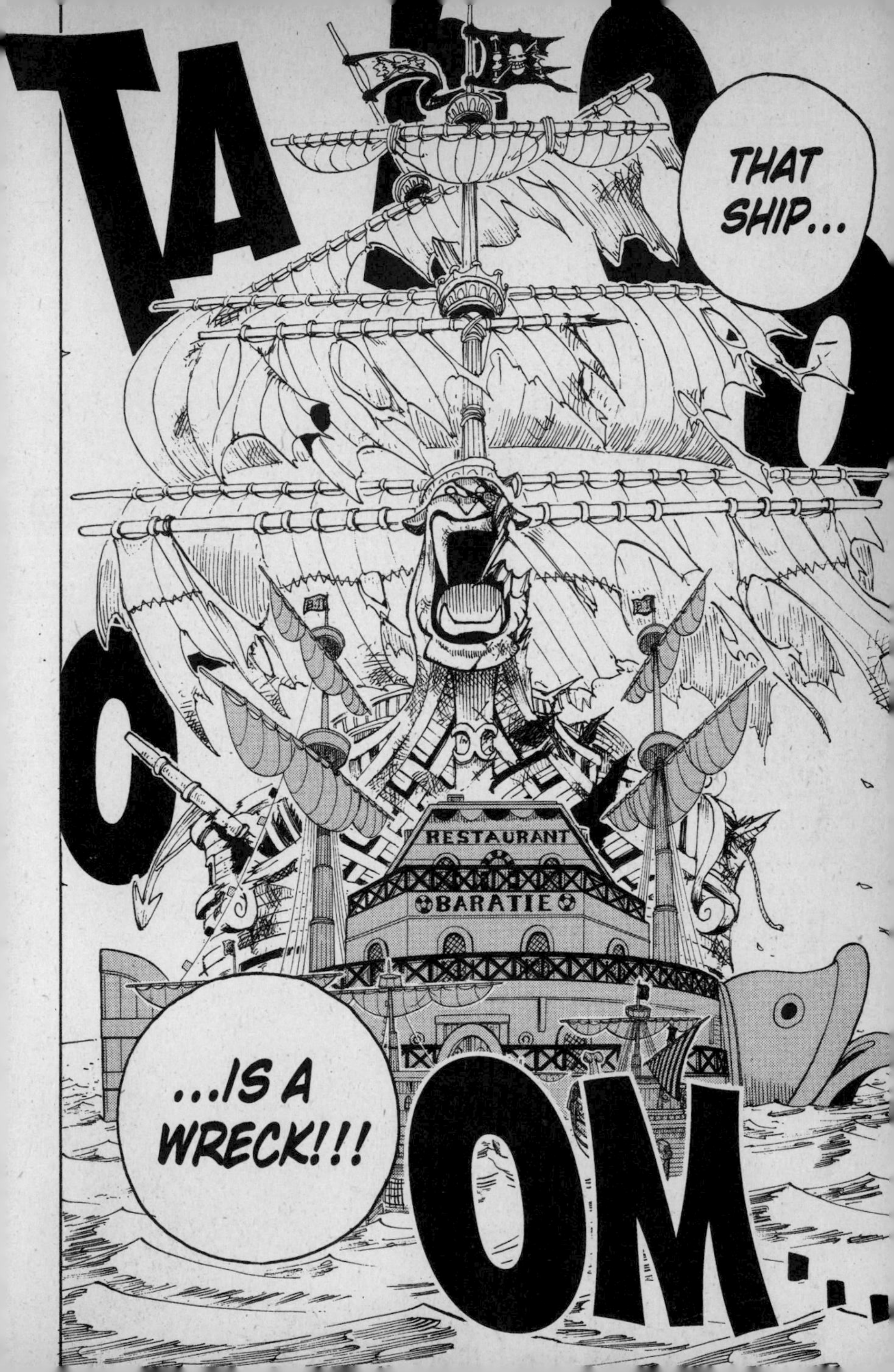
TA
THAT SHIP...
RESTAURANT
BARATIE
...IS A WRECK!!!
OM...

READ THIS WAY

A GREAT GALLEON, RAVAGED TO THAT DEGREE...
THAT WASN'T THE WORK OF MEN.
THEY MUST HAVE SAILED THROUGH A TYPHOON!

!!
WOOSH...!!
yack yack ...!!

HUH?
!?
WOOOO...
.....
!?
GASP...!

PLEASE... MAY I HAVE... SOME FOOD AND WATER?
HUFF
I'VE GOT MONEY... LOTS OF MONEY...
HUFF
DON KRIEG
Admiral of the Pirate Armada

READ THIS WAY

WHAT...?
WHO IS THAT?
PRETTY SHABBY FOR A KING.

HE LOOKS HUNGRY.
WHAT'S GOING ON?

Wobble...

FWOMP
DON KRIEG!!!
UGH...

FOOD!! WATER!! PLEASE!!
THE DON'S ON THE VERGE OF DEATH!!
IF YOU DON'T HELP HIM, HE'S DOOMED!!!

HA HA HA HA!! HOW RICH!! WHATTA LAUGH!!
DIS BUM IS THE DREADED DON KRIEG?!

THIS TIME I'VE GOT MONEY!! WE'RE CUSTOMERS!!!

!?
ALERT THE NAVY!!
THEY WON'T WANNA MISS AN OPPORTUNITY TO CATCH THIS FIEND!
DON'T FEED 'EM A CRUMB!! JUST GRAB 'EM!!

IF HE REGAINS HIS STRENGTH, THERE'S NO TELLING WHAT HE'LL DO TO US!!
HE'S A PIRATE AND A KILLER! STARVING'S TOO GOOD FOR HIM!!
HE DESERVES TO DIE, SO LET HIM!!

IF KRIEG REGAINS HIS STRENGTH, HE'LL PILLAGE THIS RESTAURANT.
DON'T EVEN GIVE HIM A CUP OF WATER!

!!
I WON'T HARM ANYONE... FEED ME AND I'LL LEAVE QUIETLY!!
huff huff
I BEG YOU... HELP ME!!!

DON KRIEG, DON'T!!
DON'T GROVEL!! THIS ISN'T YOU!!
IT'S BE-NEATH YOU!!!

PLEASE... I BEG YOU!!
LEFTOVER RICE... ANYTHING !!
huff
!!!
huff

ANY-THING!!

DON KRIEG!!!

HMPH
TRYING FOR SYMPATHY ?!
OUT OF THE WAY, PATTY!

WAK!!

!!?

HERE, GIN. HE CAN EAT THIS.

murmur

SANJI!!

!!

!

FLYING A NAVY FLAG, HE SAILS INTO PORTS AND ATTACKS BOTH TOWN AND SHIPS.

SOMETIMES HE FLIES A WHITE FLAG, THEN OPENS FIRE!!

MARINE

HE'LL STOOP TO ANYTHING TO WIN.

HIS DUPLICITY IS LEGENDARY!!!

AT FULL STRENGTH HE'LL BE UNSTOP-PABLE!!

HE SAYS HE'LL GO IF WE FEED HIM, BUT WE CAN'T TRUST HIM!!

SHIVER ....!!

THAT TWO-FACED SCOUNDREL SHOULD STARVE!!

THE WORLD WOULD BE A BETTER PLACE!!!

!!

!!!?
SKRSSH...!!
SANJI!!!

KRAK!!
AAAAGH!!
SWAP
THE FOOD WAS GOOD. MY STRENGTH IS RETURNING.

YOU SWORE YOU WOULDN'T HURT NOBODY IF I LED YOU HERE!!
YOU SAID YOU WOULDN'T, KRIEG!!!
THAT MAN SAVED OUR LIVES!!!

Q: By any chance is Gaimon my father? (Inquiry from the Ministry of Education, Science, and Culture.)

A: Darn! You found out! You tracked him down through the Ministry of Science. I didn't consider that possibility. Gaimon told me not to tell anyone, but I guess there's no way to hide it now. Fine! Go meet him! You're Gaimon's son! Leap into his arms and hug him! And while you're at it, leap into the ocean and cool your head, you little weirdo!

Q: I said to my friend, "Buggy's totally cute!" ♡and she took a step back and said, "You're weird!!" Am I weird?

A: Yes, you are weird!! But I like him too, that Buggy. But I'm not weird... I'm a special exception. Yeah, that's right.

Q: I have a request. ♡ Please give me Gaimon.♡

A: Uh... okay... but check with his son first.

Q: When an artist is drawing Chapter 10, which chapter is appearing in Shonen Jump?

A: I see... I used to be interested in these questions myself. At present, issue 46 of **Shonen Jump** (the Japanese edition) is out in the world. The **One Piece** chapter in there is Chapter 60. However, I've finished drawing Chapter 63. So a chapter emerges in the world three weeks after I've completed it.
But this is just my schedule, right now. Not everyone drawing for weekly publication does it the same way. And I might change, too. It varies.

Chapter 47:
THE DON'S OFFER

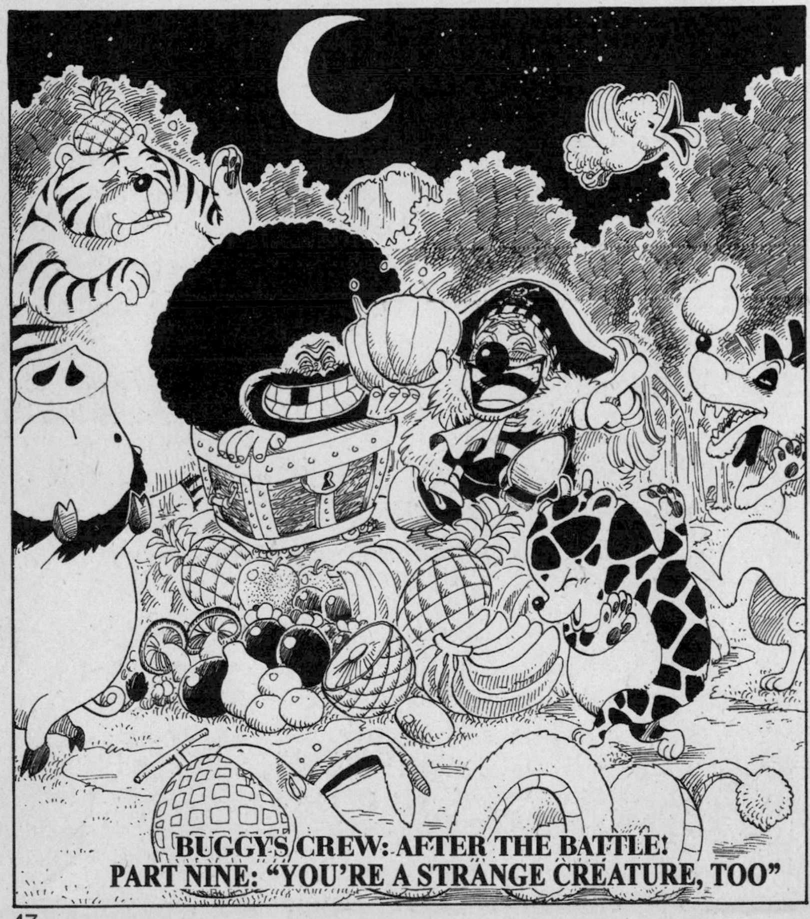

BUGGY'S CREW: AFTER THE BATTLE!
PART NINE: "YOU'RE A STRANGE CREATURE, TOO"

AAAAAAAH...!!

gasp

gasp

gasp

MY SHIP'S A WRECK.

I NEED A NEW ONE.

DOOM

WHEN I'M FINISHED WITH YOU, I'LL DUMP YOU.

I HAVE ABOUT A HUNDRED MEN ON MY SHIP WHO STILL DRAW BREATH.

THEY'RE DYING FROM WOUNDS, HUNGER AND THIRST.

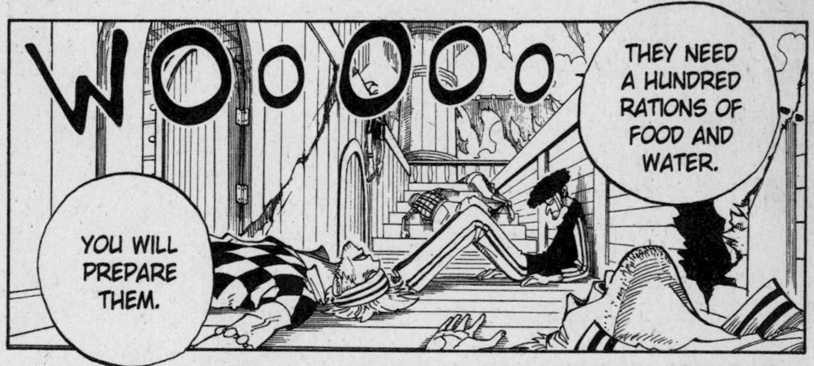

READ THIS WAY

YOU EXPECT US TO FEED A HUNDRED PIRATES?!
SO THEY'LL HAVE THE STRENGTH TO TAKE OVER OUR SHIP?!
WE REFUSE!!!

REFUSE? YOU DON'T UNDER-STAND.
IT'S NOT A REQUEST.

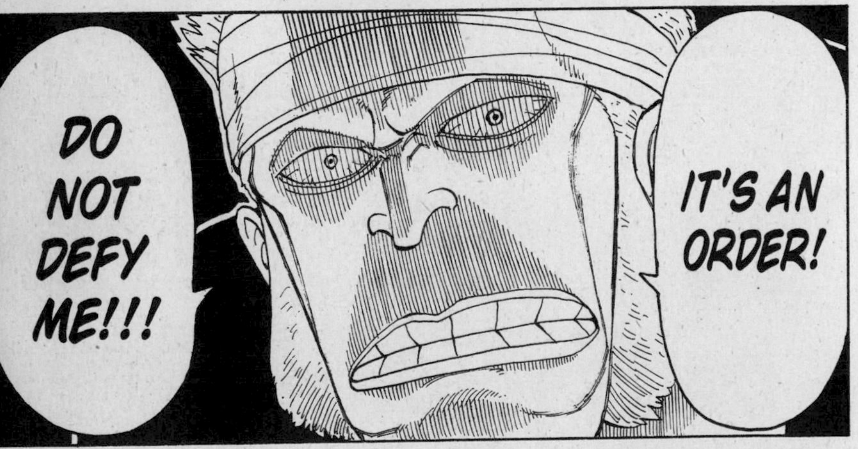
IT'S AN ORDER!
DO NOT DEFY ME!!!

GRRR!!
!!!

SORRY, SANJI... I... I NEVER MEANT--

YOU!! YOU GOT US INTO THIS MESS!!
WHERE ARE YOU GOING, SANJI?
TMP

THE KITCHEN, OF COURSE.
PTOOEY
WE'VE GOT A HUNDRED MEALS TO PREPARE.

SANJI.

THAT'S RIGHT.

SANJI?!!

WHAT?!!

KLIK...!!
!

ARE YOU KRIEG'S DOG, SANJI?
WE CAN'T LET YOU INTO THE KITCHEN.
WE'RE NOT GOING ALONG WITH THIS.
IT'S AN OUT-RAGE !!

!
IF YOU WANT TO STOP ME...
FIRE.

I KNOW...
!
...THEY'RE UNREDEEM-ABLE VILLAINS.
....!!
BUT MY JOB IS TO FEED PEOPLE, NOT TO JUDGE THEM.
IT GETS TOO COMPLICATED.

IF A MAN IS HUNGRY, I FEED HIM!!!

THAT'S A COOK'S JOB.

WHAT'S THE PROBLEM?

......!!

!!

PATTY!!

HOLD HIM DOWN.

SANJI, I KNOW YOU FEED THE PEOPLE I CHASE OFF.
MAYBE YOU'RE RIGHT TO DO THAT SOMETIMES.
BUT THIS TIME, YOU'RE WRONG!!
NOW YOU KEEP STILL. I'M GONNA DEFEND THIS RESTAURANT!!
......
!

KA-CHAK!!
YOU'VE EATEN!
HERE'S YOUR DESSERT!!!
BOOM
THE MEAT-BALL OF DOOM!!!!

KABOOM!!!

KR—AK!!

KSSSh!!
BLAST, I BUSTED THE DOORS.
CHEF'LL HAVE YOUR HIDE.

IT'S NOTHING.
A SMALL PRICE TO PAY FOR SAVING BARATIE.

WHAT ABOUT THE MEN ON KRIEG'S SHIP?

HMM...I SAY WE SMEAR BUTTER ON THE SHIP AND SET IT ON FIRE.

WOOOOOO

THAT DESSERT WAS A BIT HEAVY FOR MY TASTE.

HARDLY A FOUR-STAR MEAL.

MBAMBAM
INSOLENCE!!!!
!!!?

AAAAAAAH!!!
BAM

GUN BARRELS!! ALL OVER HIM!!
BULLETS!
...!!
NO ONE DEFIES KRIEG, YOU WORTHLESS SCUM!!
I AM STRONGER THAN ANYONE!!!
ARMS OF STEEL, STRONGER THAN ANY FLESH!!
KREEK...
A CARAPACE OF THE STRONGEST WOOTZ STEEL!!

DIAMOND FISTS TO DEMOLISH ANYTHING!!!
AND A BUILT-IN ARRAY OF WEAPONS!!!

I COMMAND 50 SHIPS AND 5,000 FIGHTING MEN!

I'VE NEVER LOST A BATTLE!! I AM THE DON OF THE PIRATE ARMADA!!!

IF I TELL YOU TO PREPARE FOOD...
...YOU'LL SHUT UP AND DO IT!!!

NO ONE DEFIES ME!!!!

!
KLUNK....
CHEF ZEFF!!

YOU WENT TO THE GRAND LINE.
BUT YOU RAN SCARED, EH?

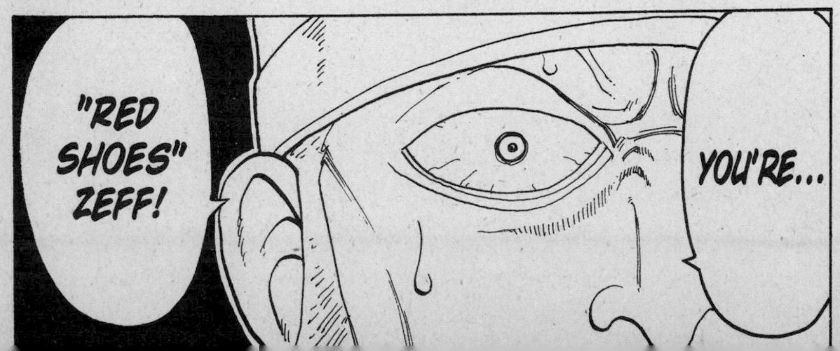

Q: What happened to the key that Chou-Chou swallowed in Volume 2?

A: It came out...with a lovely brown sheen.

Q: In a Question Corner in Volume 4, you said that Luffy's arms can stretch about 72 gum-gums, but how many meters are in a gum-gum? (Inquiry from the Ministry of Education, Science, and Culture.)

A: You again! Gaimon's son, investigating through the Ministry of Science again, eh? Meters, you ask? It can't be measured that way. Now pay attention. One gum-gum equals 10 fairy gum-gums. One fairy gum-gum equals 10 funky gum-gums. So one gum-gum equals 100 funky gum-gums, which means that Luffy's arms can stretch a whopping 7,200 funky gum-gums. Is that clear?

Q: Where are you from? It didn't say in your profile in Volume 4.

A: Kumamoto, in Kyushu. It's a nice place.

Q: How come Luffy and Zolo don't go by the names Monkey and Roronoa? Or are those their surnames?

A: That's it. Their surnames come first, Japanese style. Luffy and Zolo are their first names.

Q: Is there a mirror on Alvida's ship?

A: Ugh! Look out, her iron club will come flying! You're on your own! Man, what a dangerous question. But ... I bet there isn't a mirror. (Klang!!!) Ow!

Q: I've been reading One Piece, and I notice that sometimes mysterious characters pop up. For example, in the third panel on page 182 of ONE PIECE Volume 5, where everyone is going "murmur murmur," there's a panda-headed guy in the background. Who is it? It's bugging me so much I can't brush my teeth.

A: Brush your teeth. The dentist is scary, you know. So you found him, eh? His name is Panda Man, and he's a wrestler. I'll introduce him properly next time.

Chapter 48:
STEER CLEAR

BUGGY'S CREW: AFTER THE BATTLE!
PART 10: "FAREWELL TO FRIENDS"

"RED SHOES" ZEFF. SO YOU'RE ALIVE.
A UNIQUE PIRATE, THE CAPTAIN-COOK.

SO WHAT IF I'M ALIVE?
WHAT'S IT TO YOU?
NOW I'M A CHEF EXCLUSIVELY.

READ THIS WAY

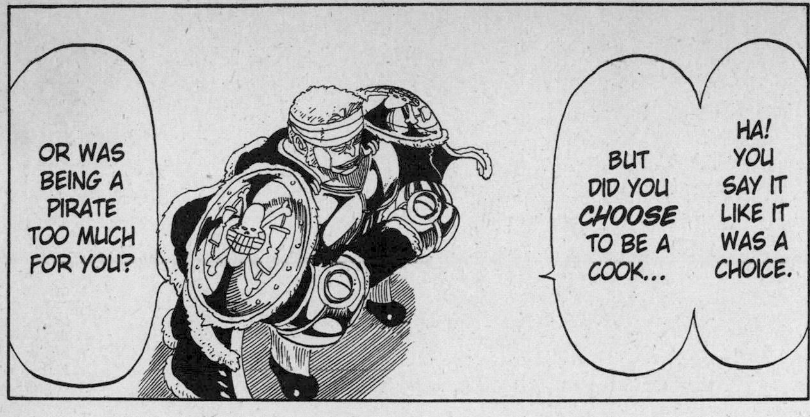
HA! YOU SAY IT LIKE IT WAS A CHOICE.
BUT DID YOU CHOOSE TO BE A COOK...
OR WAS BEING A PIRATE TOO MUCH FOR YOU?

....
LOOKS LIKE YOUR RED SHOES DAYS ARE BEHIND YOU.

"RED SHOES" ZEFF...
...MASTER OF THE DEADLY KICK, WHO NEVER USED HIS HANDS IN BATTLE.
THAT AWESOME LEG STRENGTH COULD SMASH BEDROCK...
...AND EVEN LEAVE FOOTPRINTS IN STEEL.

THE BLOOD OF YOUR ENEMIES DYED YOUR SHOES...
...HENCE YOUR UNUSUAL NICKNAME.

THEY SAY YOU DIED AT SEA.
I SEE YOU DIDN'T LOSE YOUR LIFE...
...BUT YOU DID LOSE ONE OF YOUR PRECIOUS LEGS.

....

I CAN'T FIGHT ANYMORE, BUT I CAN COOK, LONG AS I HAVE THESE TWO HANDS.
WHAT ARE YOU GETTING AT? SPIT IT OUT.

"RED SHOES" ZEFF... YOU ONCE SAILED THAT DEVIL'S NEST, THE GRAND LINE.
BUT YOU RETURNED UNSCATHED.
YOU KEPT A RECORD OF THAT VOYAGE, A WHOLE YEAR'S LOG.
GIVE ME YOUR LOG-BOOK!!!

THEN I'LL TAKE IT FROM YOU!!!
IT'S TRUE THAT I DIDN'T SUCCEED ON THE GRAND LINE!!
BUT I AM DON KRIEG, THE MIGHTIEST OF ALL!

WEAKLINGS DO WELL TO SHUN THAT DARK ROUTE.
BUT I HAD PLENTY OF STRENGTH!! SHIPS AND MEN!! AND AMBITION!!

THE ONLY THING I LACKED WAS KNOWLEDGE!!!
THAT'S WHAT STOPPED ME!!!

I JUST DIDN'T KNOW ENOUGH.
I'LL HAVE THAT LOG... AND THIS SHIP, TOO!!

YOU CAN'T HAVE IT! THIS SHIP'S ALL WE'VE GOT IN THE WORLD.
YEAH. WE'VE BEEN CAST OUT FROM EVERYWHERE ELSE.
CHEF ZEFF IS OUR SAVIOR! HE TOOK US IN WHEN NO ONE ELSE WOULD!
WE WON'T LET YOU TAKE OUR SHIP!!!

PUNY FOOLS!! NO ONE CAN DEFY ME!!!
GRARR!!
YOU'VE SEEN THAT I'M THE STRONGEST OF ALL!!
GASP!
GULP

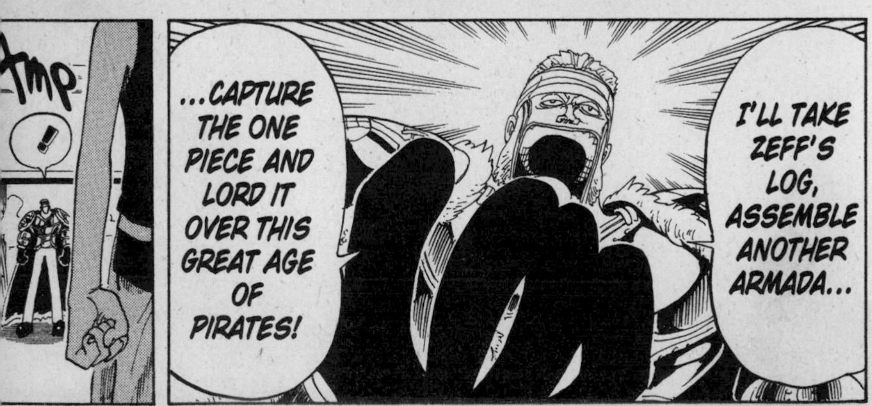
I'LL TAKE ZEFF'S LOG, ASSEMBLE ANOTHER ARMADA...
...CAPTURE THE ONE PIECE AND LORD IT OVER THIS GREAT AGE OF PIRATES!
TMP
!

HOLD IT!!

I'M GOING TO BE KING OF THE PIRATES!

READ THIS WAY

DID YOU SAY SOME-THING, BOY?
DON'T YOU WANT TO TAKE THAT BACK?
NOPE.
I WAS ONLY STATING THE FACTS.
.....

THIS ISN'T A GAME.
GRR R...

OBVIOUSLY.

?
WEREN'T YOU LISTENING? THE GRAND LINE WAS TOO MUCH EVEN FOR KRIEG!
WUSP
WUSP

CAN'T WE JUST CALL IT OFF? GOING THERE IS SUICIDE!
QUIET. STAY OUT OF THIS.
!

TIME TO FIGHT, LUFFY?

DADOOM!

I'LL LEND A HAND.

WRONG! THERE ARE TWO MORE!!
fwik!
DON'T COUNT ME IN!

DON'T BE SO COCKSURE, KID!!! I HAD A FLEET AND 5,000 MEN!
IN SEVEN DAYS, WE WERE SMASHED TO BITS IN THAT DEMON SEA!!!

!!
SEVEN DAYS?!!
KRIEG'S ARMADA WAS DESTROYED SO QUICKLY?!!
WHAT COULD HAVE DONE IT?!!

DID YOU HEAR THAT?! FIFTY SHIPS IN ONE WEEK!!
SOUNDS INTER-ESTING.

RECKLESS IMPUDENCE. BUT YOU'RE NOT FUNNY.
WATCH YOUR MOUTH OR I'LL KILL YOU RIGHT NOW!!

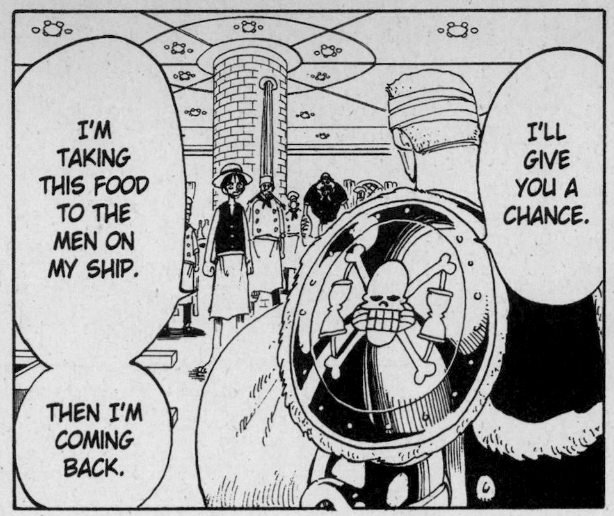
I'LL GIVE YOU A CHANCE.
I'M TAKING THIS FOOD TO THE MEN ON MY SHIP.
THEN I'M COMING BACK.

KRSH
NOW LISTEN CAREFULLY.

ANYONE WHO DOESN'T WANT TO DIE HAD BETTER BE GONE WHEN I RETURN.
ALL I WANT IS THE CAPTAIN'S LOG AND THE SHIP.

BUT IF YOU'RE EAGER TO DIE...
TOMP.
...WAIT FOR ME. I'LL BURY YOU AT SEA.
TOMP
IT'S YOUR CHOICE.
TOMP...

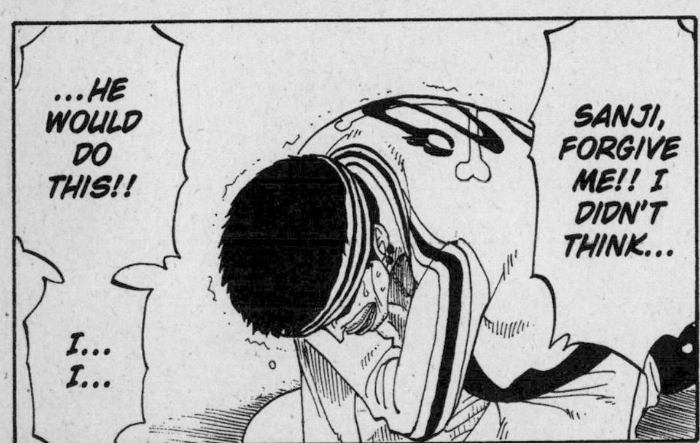
SANJI, FORGIVE ME!! I DIDN'T THINK...
...HE WOULD DO THIS!!
I... I...

....!!

IT'S NOT ALL YOUR FAULT, SWABBY.
HUH?
CHEF...
THE COOKS HELPED TO BRING THIS ON US, AS WELL.

CHEF!! ARE YOU SIDING WITH SANJI?
YOU CRAZY?!
HE'S THE GUY WHO STARTED ALL THIS TROUBLE!!
SANJI WANTS TO DESTROY YOUR PRECIOUS RESTAURANT!!
......

DON'T YOU, SANJI ?!
YOU'D DO ANYTHING TO BE THE HEAD CHEF!!
EITHER THAT OR YOU'RE INSANE. WHICH IS IT?!
!
SHUT UP, YOU EGG-PLANTS !!!

READ THIS WAY

HUH...
SO WHAT, CHEF?

IF YOU'RE GONNA KEEP MOANING...
...THEN JUST HEAD OUT THE BACK DOOR!!

....!!
krk...

I'LL STAY AND FIGHT.
I CAN'T STAND TO LET KRIEG HAVE HIS WAY.
ME NEITHER! THIS RESTAURANT IS MY HOME!
YEAH! I GOT NOWHERE ELSE TO GO!

WHAT? ARE YOU FOOLS?!
YOU SAW WHAT KRIEG CAN DO!! YOU'D BETTER RUN!!
GIN...
!

LISTEN TO ME.
AS A COOK, I CONSIDER IT MY DUTY TO FEED THE HUNGRY.

BUT SOON I'LL BE FACING PLUNDERERS WITH FULL STOMACHS.

TUMP

SO IF I HAVE TO BEAT YOUR MATES TO DEATH, DON'T COMPLAIN.

READ THIS WAY

SEE? HE'S TOUGH, HUH?
WHO CARES?! WE GOTTA GET OUTTA HERE!!
flap flap
RELAX. THEY'RE WOUNDED AND STARVING.

YEAH. BESIDES, I'VE GOT TO FIGHT KRIEG.
HE'S A POWERFUL RIVAL. I'LL HAVE TO TAKE HIM DOWN SOMETIME.

BY THE WAY, GIN...
AYE?
YOU SAID YOU DIDN'T KNOW ANYTHING ABOUT THE GRAND LINE.
BUT YOU'VE BEEN THERE!

.....!!
I KNOW NOTHING. IT'S ALL A CRAZY FOG. SOMETHING HAPPENED ON OUR SEVENTH DAY OUT.
BUT WAS IT A DREAM OR REALITY? IT'S ALL MIXED UP IN MY HEAD.
...HE APPEARED SO SUD-DENLY...

JUST... ONE... MAN.

HOW COULD ONE MAN SCUPPER 50 SHIPS?!!

BEFORE WE KNEW IT...
...OUR SHIPS WERE SINKING, ONE AFTER THE OTHER!
IF THAT STORM HADN'T COME UP...
...HE'D HAVE SENT THE FLAGSHIP TO THE BOTTOM, TOO!

I'M NOT SURE HOW MANY SHIPS SURVIVED...
IT WAS TERRIBLE... I CAN'T BELIEVE IT WAS REAL!!
I DON'T WANT TO REMEMBER THAT MAN!

THAT MAN WITH THE PIERCING HAWK EYES, EYES THAT COULD KILL WITH A GLANCE!!!!
WHAT ?!!

Chapter 49: STORM

KRIEG'S ARMADA WAS WRECKED BY ONE MAN!?

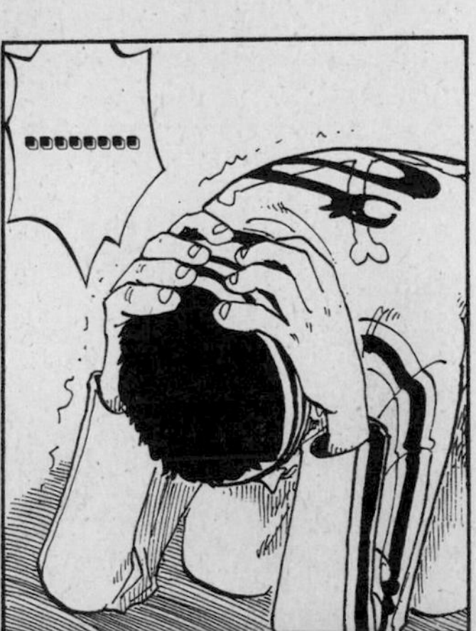

HAW...
HAWK-EYE!!?

YOU SAID HIS EYES...
...WERE LIKE A HAWK'S. THAT'S PROOF ENOUGH.
BUT WHAT HE DID TO YOUR SHIPS...
IT HAD TO BE *HIM*!!

HAW... HAWK...
HAWK-EYE!?

WHO'S HE?
wump
BEATS ME.

HE'S THE MAN I'VE BEEN LOOKING FOR.
WHAT !?
JOHNNY SAID HE COMES HERE.

DON'T KNOW ABOUT OLD "HAWK-EYE"...
...BUT "OLD RED-EYES" WAS HERE.
AYE, HE DRANK SO MUCH WINE HIS EYES TURNED RED.
THEN THE FOOL CAUGHT FIRE AND EXPLODED!
YEAH, WHAT A SIGHT.

...EVEN THAT HAWK-EYE YOU WERE HUNTING GOES THERE.
...!!
THAT SEA SNAKE! HE LIED TO ME!!

JOHNNY? WHAT'D HE DO?
AW, NOTHING.

SO HE BEAT THE WHOLE ARMADA.
DID YOU DO SOME-THING TO MAKE HIM MAD?
NOT THAT I KNOW OF! HE JUST ATTACKED!
MAYBE YOU INTERRUPTED HIS NAP.

THAT'S NOT FUNNY!! HE MURDERED MY CREWMATES!!

CALM DOWN. I WASN'T JOKING.
THAT'S THE KIND OF PLACE THE GRAND LINE IS.

?
ANYTHING CAN HAPPEN THERE, EH?

WOO-HOO! I'VE GOT GOOSE-BUMPS!!
shake shake!
A PLACE WHERE ANY-THING CAN HAPPEN!!
PLEASE! FOR ONCE, THINK OF THE DANGER!!

NOW I KNOW WHERE I HAVE TO GO.
TO THE GRAND LINE.
THAT'S WHERE I'LL FIND *HIM*!!!

......

YOU'RE FOOLS. YOU'LL BOTH BE KILLED AS SOON AS YOU GET THERE.
!
TRUE ENOUGH... BUT DON'T INSULT US.
?

THE DAY I DECIDED TO BE THE WORLD'S GREATEST SWORDSMAN, I GAVE MYSELF UP FOR DEAD.
NOBODY CALLS ME A FOOL BUT ME. I HAVE MY REASONS.

RIGHT OUT THERE, THEM SEA-WOLVES ARE REVIVING THEMSELVES...

...ABOARD PIRATE ADMIRAL DON KRIEG'S GALLEON!!!

DEY'RE THE MOST SAVAGE PIRATES IN THE EASTERN SEAS!!!

IF YOU WANNA DREAM, DO IT AFTER THIS CRISIS IS OVER!!!

WOOO
OOOO

MUNCH
MUNCH
CHOMP CHOMP CHOMP

AHHH!!
AH-ROOO!!!
....

ROOARR

WE'RE SAVED!!!

READ THIS WAY

!!
HUH!!?

WHAT'S THIS?
WHY THE FROWNS?

RETURN?
TO CERTAIN DEATH!?

BANG!
UGH!!!
!!?

ANY-BODY ELSE?
OR ARE WE IN AGREEMENT?

AYE...
RAAAAR!!!

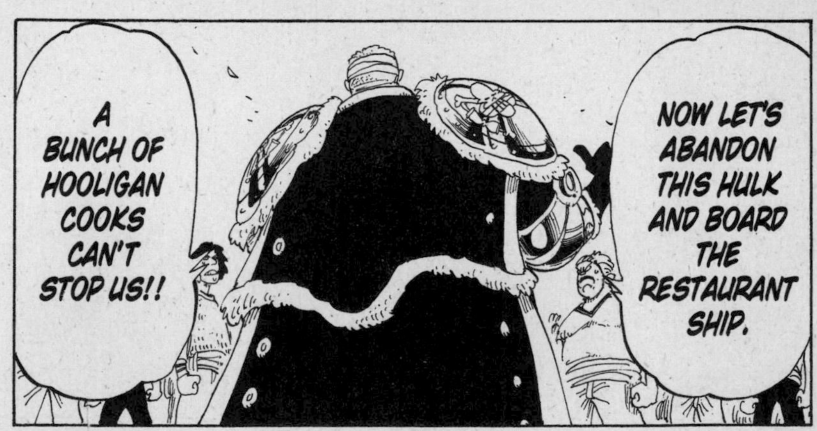
NOW LET'S ABANDON THIS HULK AND BOARD THE RESTAURANT SHIP.
A BUNCH OF HOOLIGAN COOKS CAN'T STOP US!!

OOOOO
THEY'RE COMING! THAT'S THEIR BATTLE CRY!
WE MUST DEFEND OUR RESTAURANT !!!
OOOOO
STAND DOWN, YOU COOKS!!!

KRAS
RESTAURANT
BARATIE

WHOA!!
!!?
TOMP!
WHAT WAS THAT !!?
!?
WHAT HAPPENED !!?
RAAAAR

DON KRIEG!!! THE SHIP!!!
WAAAAAH!
IT'S LISTING!!!
GRAAA
RAAR
LISTING? MY FLAGSHIP GALLEON!!? BUT...
...HOW COULD THAT BE??

NAMI, JOHNNY AND YOSAKU ARE ON OUR SHIP!!
tmp tmp!!
IT MAY BE TOO LATE!!!
WEIGH ANCHOR!!!
WAAAAH
THEY WANT OUR RESTAURANT!!!
YES, SIR!
BROTHER!!
BROTHER!!!
SPLASH
SPLASH
SPLASH
YOSAKU!! JOHNNY!! YOU OKAY!?
WHERE'S OUR SHIP!? WHERE'S NAMI!?
SORRY, BROTHER ZOLO!!! THEY'RE...
THEY'RE GONE!!!

SISTER NAMI !!
SO LONG! GIVE THE OTHERS MY BEST!
TELL THEM I HOPE WE MEET AGAIN! ♡
SHE SAILED OFF WITH ALL THE TREASURE !!!!

WHAT !!!?
SHE TOOK THE SHIP !!!?

......!

UH-OH...
WOOOOO
IT'S HIM!!

Q: There's gum-gum fruit, scatter-scatter fruit, and other kinds of devil fruit. I thought of a new one: "icky-icky fruit." It makes you so gross that nothing wants to come near you. VERY useful.

A: Okay, you eat it first.

Q: I think all of Oda Sensei's drawings of Buggy show him with his mouth open. I'd like to see one with his lips closed.

Q: When you were asked about Nami's measurements, you said you'd reveal them. When are you going to keep your promise!?

A: Heh Heh. I recruited a specialist to help me. His keen eye is infallible. Able to guess a girl's dimensions with just one look, he's the shady cook Sanji!!

Sanji: Hi, crap-jerk! I'm not a "shady" cook, I'm a "ladies" cook!! But you did right to call me. Leave this to me. Nami is lovely, isn't she? Great sense of style, too. Looks like... 34-22-34! Yes, definitely!! Oh, she's so cute. I hear she's a thief, but I like her...

A: There, I kept my promise. Thanks, Sanji. (krak) Owwww!

Nami: What do you think you're doing?

A: Nami! Darn! Were we wrong?

Nami: No, you were right. Not that it matters. It's not like things are gonna change size. See you later... (tmp tmp)

A: Hey!! She stole my wallet!! Aaaaaah!

Chapter 50:
A PARTING OF WAYS

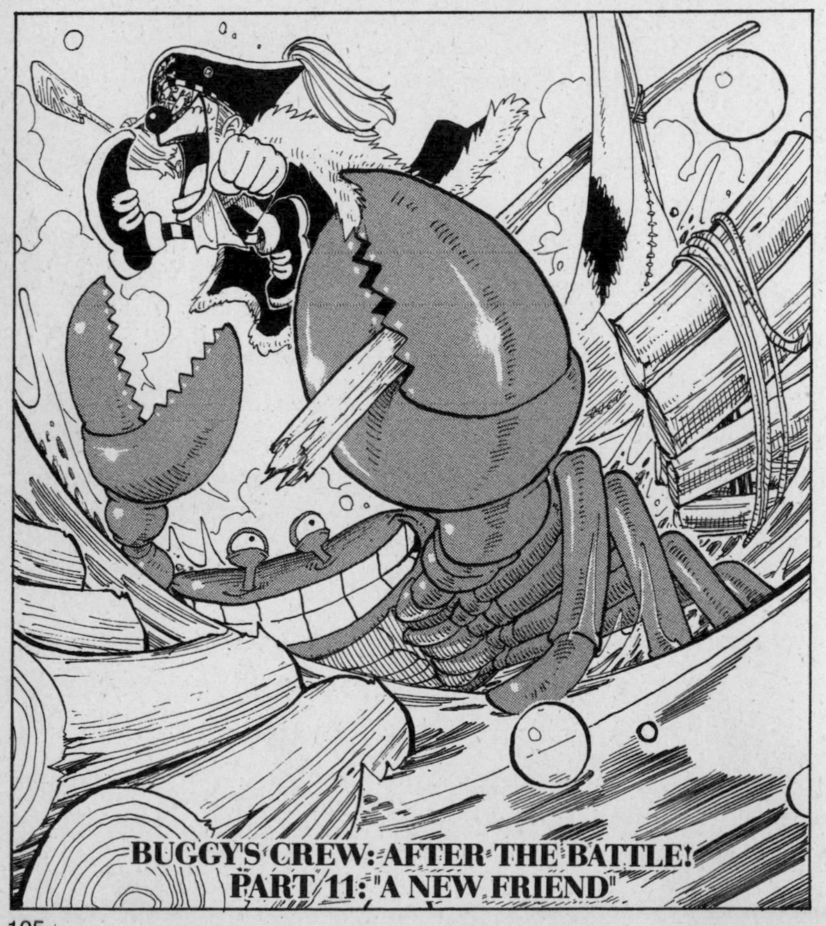

BUGGY'S CREW: AFTER THE BATTLE!
PART 11: "A NEW FRIEND"

WOOOOO
WAAAAA!!

!
WHY DO YOU KEEP STARING AT THAT BOUNTY LIST?
WHAT?
NO REASON.
THOSE ARE ALL BIG-BOUNTY PIRATES...
...BUT YOU'D BETTER GIVE THAT ONE A WIDE BERTH.
HE DISAPPEARED A WHILE BACK.
SEEMS HE'S BACK TO HIS WICKED WAYS...
hmph
hmph

AH.
STILL, A 20 MILLION-BERRY BOUNTY IS HARD TO PASS UP!
THAT WAS ONE ROUGH SEA-DOG.
EVEN WE WERE A FROG'S HAIR FROM BEING KILLED.
tmp tmp
HUH?
SISTER NAMI! THAT'S THE TREASURE FROM OUR SHIP!
I KNOW! I BROUGHT IT OVER!
HUH? BUT WE'RE NOT PLANNING TO STAY ON THIS SHIP!
TMP TMP...
COULD YOU BOYS LOOK THE OTHER WAY FOR A SEC?
HUH?
I WANT TO CHANGE CLOTHES!
DON'T LOOK, PLEEEASE?
CH-CHANGE CLOTHES!? NOW?
UH! SURE! WE WON'T LOOK!
GULP
BUMP BUMP BUMP BUMP

SISTER NAMI'S AS BRAZEN AS SHE LOOKS.
gulp
THERE'S NO HARM IN PEEKING A *LITTLE*, RIGHT?
YEAH... A LITTLE PEEK WON'T HURT...
JUST TWO SECONDS.
HUH?

WHOA!?

KER-PLASH!
HEY!!
WHAT'RE YOU DOING, SISTER NAMI!!?
SPLASH

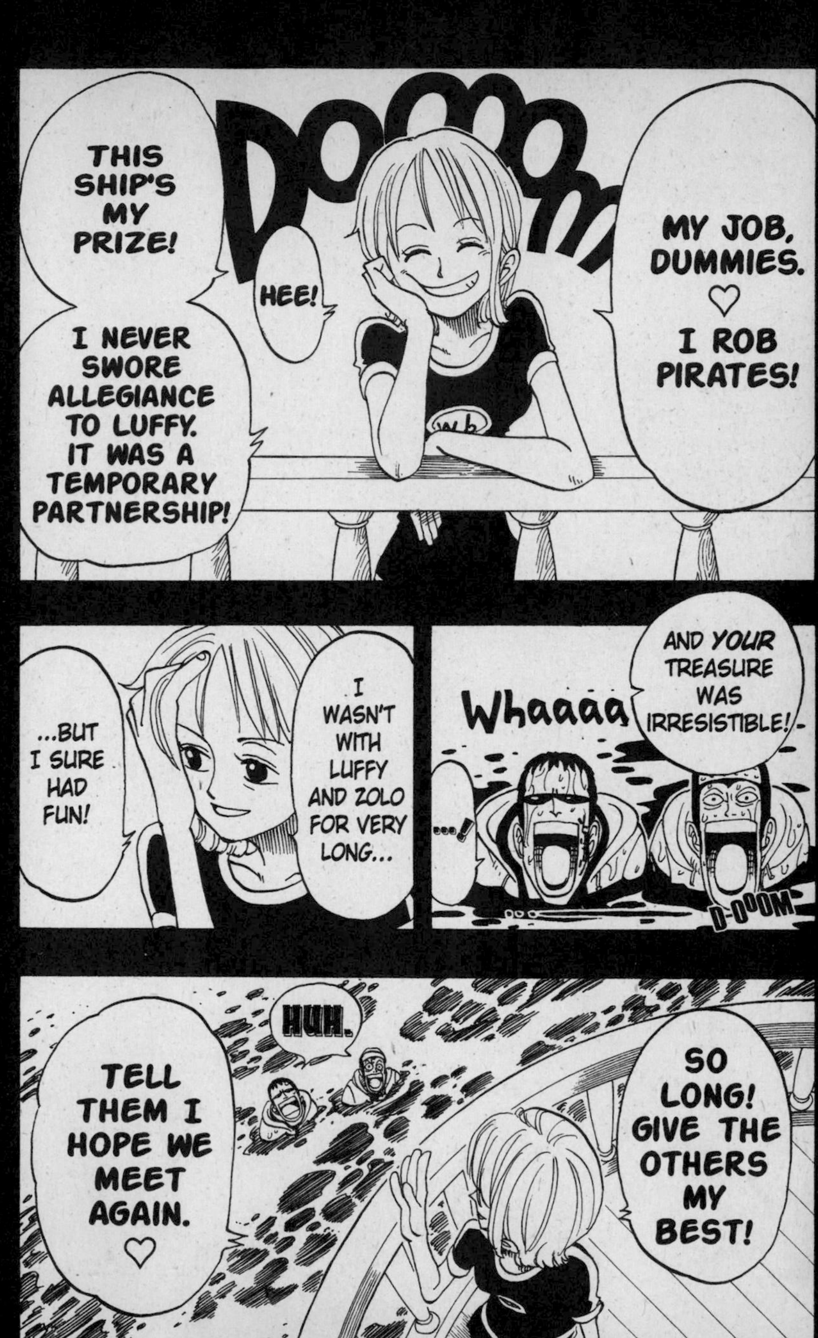
MY JOB, DUMMIES. ♡
I ROB PIRATES!
DOOOOM
HEE!
THIS SHIP'S MY PRIZE!
I NEVER SWORE ALLEGIANCE TO LUFFY. IT WAS A TEMPORARY PARTNERSHIP!
AND YOUR TREASURE WAS IRRESISTIBLE!
Whaaaa
...!
D-OOOM
I WASN'T WITH LUFFY AND ZOLO FOR VERY LONG...
...BUT I SURE HAD FUN!
SO LONG! GIVE THE OTHERS MY BEST!
HUH.
TELL THEM I HOPE WE MEET AGAIN. ♡

GIVE US BACK OUR TREASURE !!
IT WAS OUR DUTY TO GUARD THE SHIP!!!
YOU CAN'T DO THIS TO US, NAMI!!!
AAH!! WHAT NOW!?
KABOOM!!
!!
SHE ABANDONED US IN OUR TIME OF NEED!!
DARN THAT WENCH!! WE SHOULD'VE KNOWN HER GOOD BEHAVIOR WAS JUST AN ACT!!!
WHAK!
BUMP!!
AND THAT'S HOW SHE GOT AWAY!!

HEY! I CAN STILL SEE THE SHIP!!
WHAT!?

IT'S THE MERRY GO!!

YOSAKU! JOHNNY! WHERE'S YOUR SHIP!?
IT'S ANCHORED NEARBY.

ZOLO! USOPP!!
FORGET HER. WHY GO CHASING AFTER THAT LITTLE THIEF?
BUT WHAT ABOUT THE SHIP!?
KAYA'S SHIP?

NO! NAMI'S GOING TO BE OUR NAVIGATOR...
...AND NOBODY ELSE!!!

READ THIS WAY

DON KRIEG!!! IT'S HIM!!!

THE DEVIL WHO SANK OUR SHIPS!!!

READ THIS WAY

DAT'S HIM? THE FIEND WHO SANK 50 SHIPS...
...SINGLE-HANDEDLY !?
THAT'S THE ONE WHO BLASTED KRIEG'S SHIP JUST NOW!?
HE LOOKS HUMAN ENOUGH...
I DON'T SEE ANY SPECIAL WEAPON...

HIS SPECIAL WEAPON IS ON HIS BACK!

WHAT!? HOW!?
HE WRECKED THE HUGE GALLEON WITH A SWORD!?

YES! HAWK-EYE IS A MASTER SWORDS-MAN.
HE IS THE GREATEST SWORDS-MAN IN THE WORLD!

DOOM
"HAWK-EYE" MIHAWK
The Greatest Swordsman
in the World

......!!
shiver shiver
WE'RE DOOMED...
shake shake

YOU MONSTER!! WHY DO YOU KEEP PICKING ON US!?
.....

FOR FUN.
!!!
BAM
BAM
FOR FUN !!!?
!!?
shing...

WHOOSH...

HE DEFLECTED THE BULLETS WITH HIS SWORD.
NO. SHOOTING AT HIM IS USELESS.
!
WHAT!!? YOU... MISSED!!

swff!
WITHOUT SUBTLETY, A SWORD IS BUT AN IRON BAR.

HUH!? WHO ARE YOU!?
I'VE NEVER SEEN SUCH SUBTLE SWORD-WORK.

YOU SPLIT THIS GALLEON WITH THAT SWORD?

OF COURSE.

I SEE.
THEN YOU ARE THE GREATEST.

!
TH-THREE SWORDS!?
COULD THIS GUY BE...

I WENT TO SEA TO FIND YOU!!
WHY?
FWUP

LOOKING FOR SOME FUN?
THEN FIGHT ME.

TO BE THE GREATEST.
erk

WHOA!!
THE THREE-SWORD STYLE!! THAT'S ZOLO!! RORONOA ZOLO!!!
WHAT!?
...THE PIRATE HUNTER...
THAT GUY?

THERE'S NO TIME FOR THIS! THE SHIP'S ALMOST OUT OF SIGHT!
BROTHER...
....

PATHETIC.
WEAKLING.

IF YOU'RE A COMPETENT SWORDSMAN, YOU DON'T NEED TO CROSS SWORDS...

...TO KNOW THAT I FAR SURPASS YOUR PUNY SKILLS.

DOES THE COURAGE TO POINT YOUR BLADE AT ME COME FROM CONFIDENCE...

WHAT A SWELL BUNCH OF GUYS.

IF WE MEET AGAIN...
...I HOPE THEY'LL LET ME SAIL WITH THEM.

PLIP
PLIP
I HOPE WE MEET AGAIN!!

I CAN'T WAIT TO BE FREE...
PLIP
PLIP
BELLE-MÈRE !!!

Q: Did women pirates really exist?

A: Yes. But there were times when it was considered unlucky to have a woman aboard a ship, so some dressed as men to become pirates. Two female pirates were Mary Read and Anne Bonny, who were said to have fought more bravely than men. Captain Alvida was named after the Viking queen Alvida, who formed an all-woman pirate crew.

Q: A little while ago there was a manga called ***Oni ga Kitarite,*** by Shinga-Gin, and some of the panels really look like they were drawn by you. By any chance did you work as an assistant on it?

A: I get questions like this a lot, so I'd like to resolve this once and for all. Hiroyuki Takei, Shinga-Gin, Mikio Ito and I were all assistants together on ***Rurouni Kenshin***. So yes, I have helped out on brother Shinga-Gin's manga. And while I'm at it, Shinya Suzuki, who recently debuted in **Jump** (the Japanese version), is also from the old "Ruro" gang, and he's helped on ***One Piece*** a number of times. That's how we all know each other. Okay?

Q: The other day I tried to get my hair cut like Zolo's, but the barber just shaved it off. What should I say to get my hair cut like Zolo's?

A: Say, "Please give me a Strong Manly Spirit Cut."

Q: In chapter 37, was the sailor who captured the fake "Kuro of the Thousand Plans" Captain Axe-Hand Morgan? My friend and I think it looks like him.

A: It is Morgan. He was a sergeant then, but after that incident he was promoted to lieutenant-commander. Then he muscled his way up to Captain and was given command of a Navy base. I suspect that when Kuro looked deep into Morgan's eyes, he probably sensed a kindred spirit of some kind.

Chapter 51:
ZOLO OVERBOARD

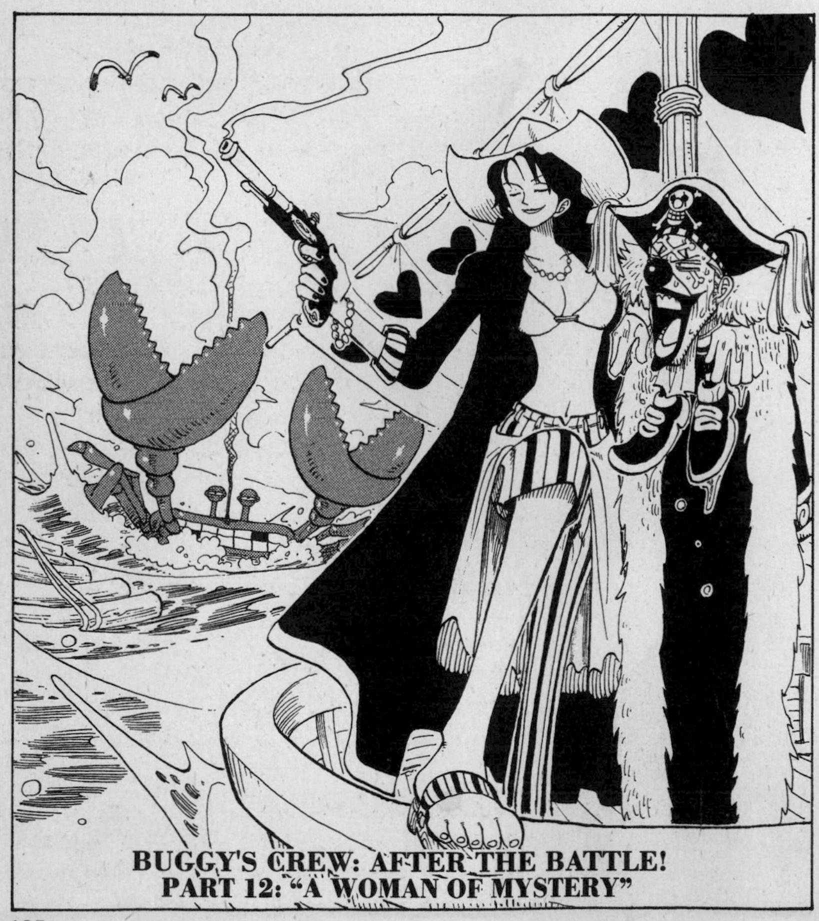

BUGGY'S CREW: AFTER THE BATTLE!
PART 12: "A WOMAN OF MYSTERY"

DA- DOOM!!

WE MEET AT LAST.
ACTUALLY, SOONER THAN I THOUGHT...

HOW FUTILE.

THE GREATEST SWORDS-MAN IN THE WORLD...

...AND ZOLO THE PIRATE HUNTER!!

WHAT'S THAT FOR?

fwip

I'M NOT THE KIND OF FOOL WHO HUNTS RABBITS WITH A CANNON.

YOU MAY HAVE A REPUTATION, BUT YOU'RE STILL JUST A BUNNY.

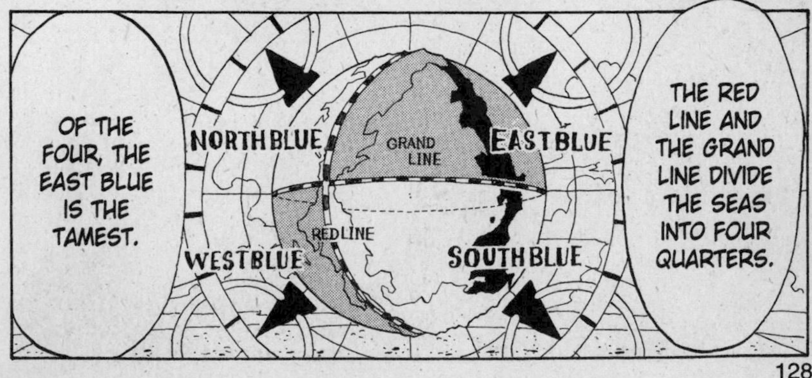
THE RED LINE AND THE GRAND LINE DIVIDE THE SEAS INTO FOUR QUARTERS.
OF THE FOUR, THE EAST BLUE IS THE TAMEST.
NORTH BLUE
GRAND LINE
EAST BLUE
RED LINE
WEST BLUE
SOUTH BLUE

TOMP!!

YOU'LL FEEL STUPID WHEN I KILL YOU !!!

YOU'RE A LITTLE FROG, CROAKING IN YOUR PUDDLE.

TIME YOU LEARNED HOW BIG THE WORLD IS.

ONI--!!!

KLANG
--GIRI
!!!!
!!?
UNH...

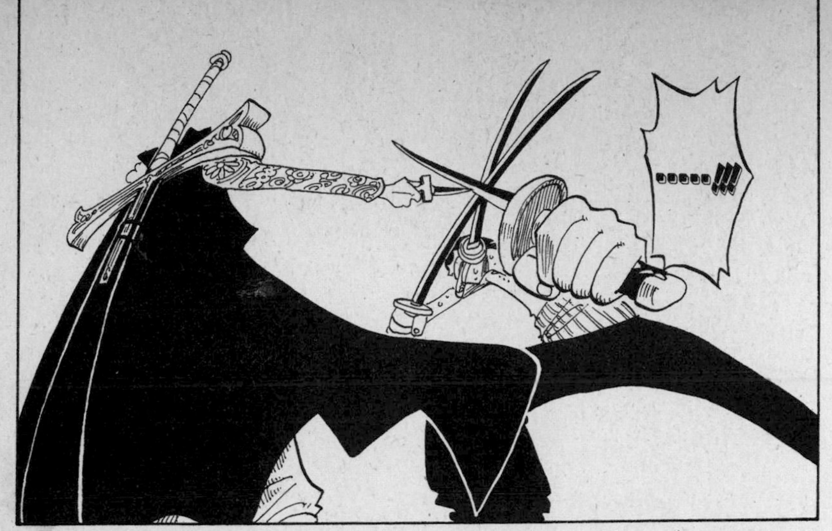

.....!!!

ZOLO?

HE STOPPED BROTHER ZOLO'S ONIGIRI DEMON CUT!!!
BUT THAT MOVE NEVER FAILS!!

IT WON'T BUDGE! NOBODY'S EVER COUNTERED MY ONIGIRI BEFORE, BUT HE DID IT WITH THAT TOY...

INCREDIBLE...
THIS CAN'T BE HAPPENING!

WE CAN'T BE THIS UNEQUAL!!

RAAAAAAR !!!
AM I REALLY SUCH A LITTLE FROG!?
KLANG
KLANG
KLANG
KLANG!!
WUMP!!
RAAR !!
THE GULF BETWEEN US CAN'T BE THIS GREAT!!
GRAAAR !!!
GRRP!

BROTHER ZOLO!! DON'T LET HIM BEAT YOU!!!
BROTHER !!!

SUCH HEAVY-HANDED SWORD PLAY...
KLANK
KLANG
GI!!
KLAN

HE'S FENDING OFF RORONOA ZOLO'S THREE-SWORD ATTACK WITH THAT TOOTHPICK !?
KLANG
KLANG!
KLANK
KLANK
KLANG
KLANG!
KLANK

TO BE COUNTERED BY A TOY!
I DIDN'T COME ALL THIS WAY TO LOSE.
KLANG
KLANG
KLANK!!

I CAME TO WIN!!!!
YOU'RE LUCKY YOU'RE A BOY, ZOLO.
I WANNA BE THE GREATEST SWORDS-MAN TOO !!

SOMEDAY, ONE OF US WILL BE THE GREATEST SWORDSMAN EVER!!
WE'LL FIGHT EACH OTHER FOR THE TITLE!
IT'S A PROM-ISE!
I MUST DEFEAT THIS MAN!!!
I'LL HAVE TO KEEP THE PROMISE FOR BOTH OF US.
I'M GOING TO BECOME SUCH A GREAT MASTER SWORDSMAN THAT MY NAME WILL BE KNOWN EVEN IN HEAVEN!!!

AAAAH!!
Waa Waa
IT'S THE PIRATE HUNTER ZOLO!!!

YOU MADE THOSE CUTTHROATS SCREAM WITH TERROR!
WE'RE YOSAKU AND JOHNNY, BOUNTY HUNTERS!!
WE'RE IMPRESSED BY YOUR SKILL!! LET'S PARTNER UP!!
DA-DOOM!!

WHAT DRIVES YOU?
WHY DO YOU FIGHT SO HARD WHEN YOU CANNOT WIN?
YOU'RE A WEAKLING...
!

OUR BROTHER'S NOT A WEAKLING, BUZZARD EYE!!!!
I'LL TEACH YOU A LESSON. THAT MAN IS...
STOP! STAY OUT OF IT, YOSAKU AND JOHNNY!!!

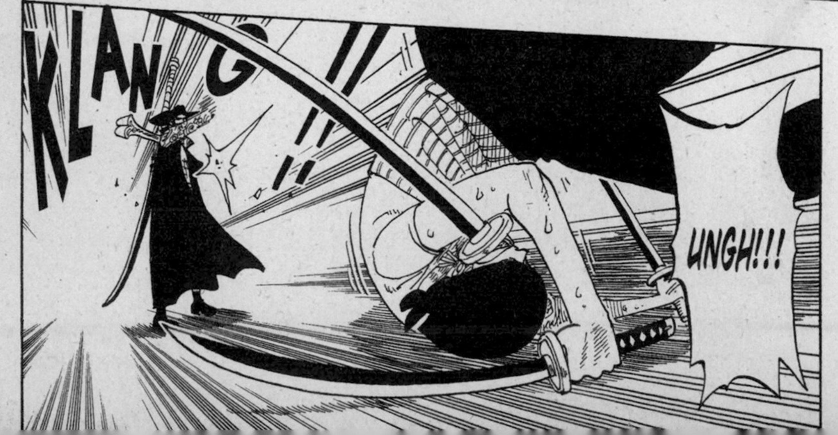

TIGER...
WOOOO
FOOSH!!
THE WORLD'S GREATEST SWORDSMAN!! THE KING OF THE PIRATES NEEDS HIM...
HE HAS TO JOIN MY CREW!!!
...HUNT!!!
HYAH!!
GREATEST IN THE WORLD...

SHUNK!!

!

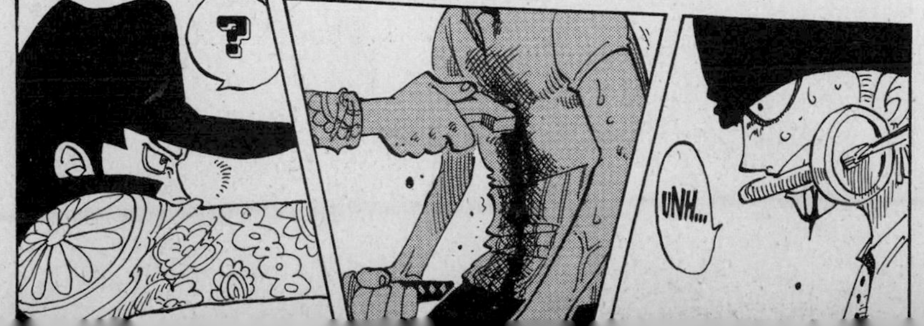

UGH
plip plip...

YOU WANT YOUR GUTS CUT OUT?
WHY DON'T YOU RETREAT?

I... CAN'T...
IF I RETREAT EVEN ONE STEP...
plop plop
...MY VOW, MY AMBITION... EVERYTHING I CARE ABOUT... WILL BE SHATTERED.
AND ALL MY DREAMS WILL BE LOST FOREVER.

YES.
THAT'S DEFEAT.

HEH...SO I CAN'T RETREAT.
THROB THROB...

EVEN IF IT MEANS DEATH?

I PREFER DEATH TO DEFEAT.

WHAT STRENGTH OF SPIRIT!!!
HE'D RATHER DIE THAN GIVE UP.

!
shluk...
BOY... SPEAK YOUR NAME.

huff
RORONOA ZOLO.
DOOM!!
huff

READ THIS WAY

HE'S DRAWN IT!!!
THE SWORD THAT SPLIT THE SHIP!!!

THIS IS MY LAST CHANCE... IT'S WIN OR DIE...
GREATEST IN THE WORLD... OR DEATH!!!
OOOO

DIE!!!

....!!!
BROTHER, PLEASE!! GIVE UP!!!

THREE-SWORD STYLE-- SECRET MOVE!!!
SHOOM
!

THREE THOUSAND WORLDS !!!!
I'VE LOST...
IT'S OVER...
......!!
KLANK...
THAT'S THE STRONGEST IN THE WORLD!!!
I NEVER FORESAW THIS...
KOFF

FWIP...

!

WHAT ARE YOU...

WOUNDS ON THE BACK...

heh

...ARE A SWORDSMAN'S SHAME.

MAGNIFICENT.

SWASH!!!

ZOLO!!!

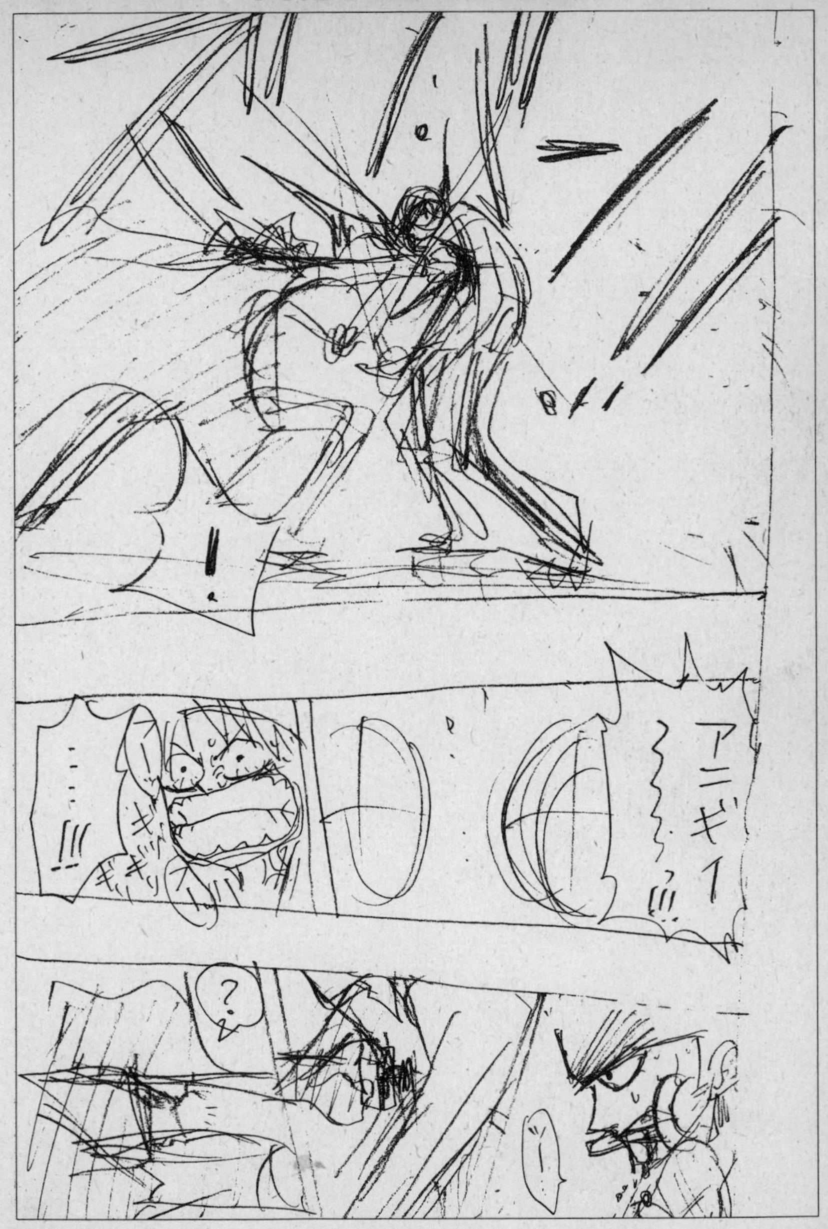
アニギイ
!!!
?

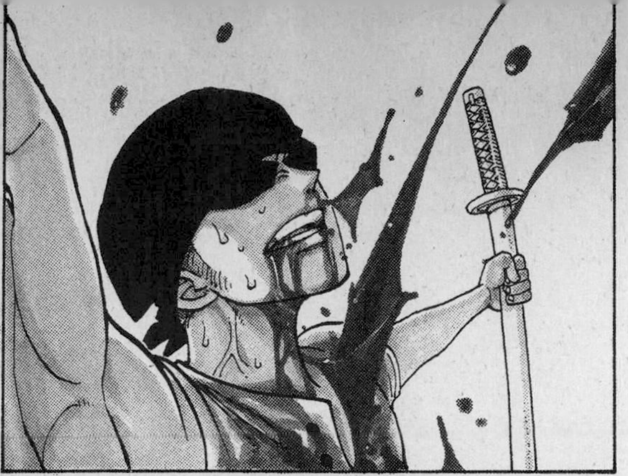

DON'T BE IN A HURRY TO DIE...

YOUNG WARRIOR !!

Chapter 52: THE OATH

Chapter 52: THE OATH

ONE
ONE PIECE

ZOLO !!!
WAAAAAAH!!
WHY!?
BROTHER !!!
EVEN THE PIRATE HUNTER ZOLO IS NO MATCH FOR HIM!!!
THERE'S A TASTE OF THE GRAND LINE!!!

IT'S EASY!!
ABANDON YOUR STUPID DREAM!!

SPLASH!!
SHINK

DARN YOU !!!

TOMP!!

BROTHER !!!

SPLA

SH!!

DARN YOU !!!

VREEN

NG!!

WAP!

!

!!?
WHAT THE HECK!!?
MUR MUR!!
GRAAAAAH!!!
SHI!!!
THE STRAW HAT BRAT!!!
HE HAS THE POWERS OF THE DEVIL FRUIT!!!

READ THIS WAY

THE YOUNG SWORDS-MAN'S CREWMATE.
YOU DID WELL...
WOOOO
TO LET HIM FIGHT HIS OWN BATTLE TO THE END!!!
WOOSH
WHAM!!?
KREEK
UNH...
KREEK
THWIP!!
UMPH!!

I LEFT HIM ALIVE.

DON'T WORRY.
!
SWUMP...!

BROTHER!! BROTHER!! SPEAK TO US!!!
SPLASH!!
ZOLO !!?

GASP!!
ZOLO!
C'MON!! GET HIM ABOARD!!

READ
THIS
WAY

MY NAME IS DRACULE MIHAWK!!
DOOM
IT'S TOO SOON FOR YOU TO DIE.

DISCOVER YOUR-SELF.
HURRY!
PUT SALVE ON HIS WOUNDS!!
SEE THE WORLD!!

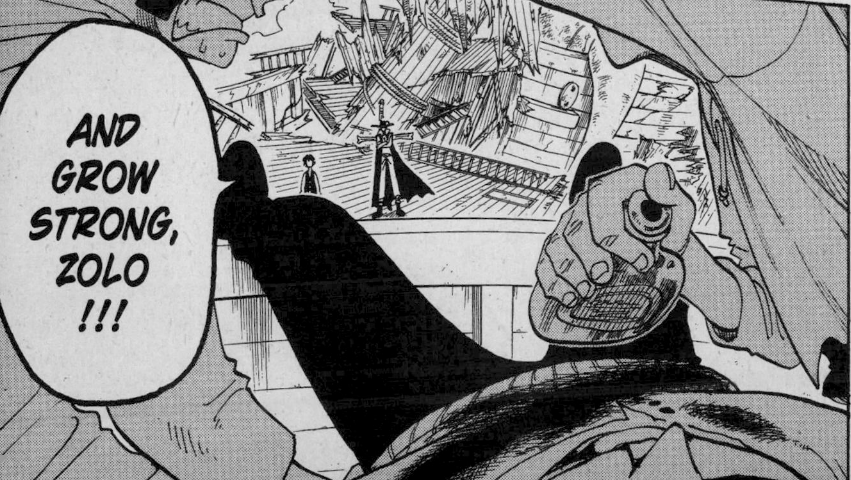
AND GROW STRONG, ZOLO!!!

STRIVE WITH YOUR WHOLE HEART AND MIND TO BEST THIS BLADE, FIERCE ONE!!!

STRIVE TO SURPASS ME, RORONOA ZOLO!!!

BROTHER!! BROTHER, SPEAK TO US!!

WHY WOULD HAWK-EYE MIHAWK SAY SOMETHING LIKE THAT?

LAD, WHAT IS YOUR GOAL?
TO BE KING OF THE PIRATES!

YOU TREAD A PERILOUS PATH.
EVEN MORE PERILOUS THAN TRYING TO SURPASS ME.

I DON'T CARE!!!
THAT'S WHAT I'M GOING TO BE!!!
NYAH

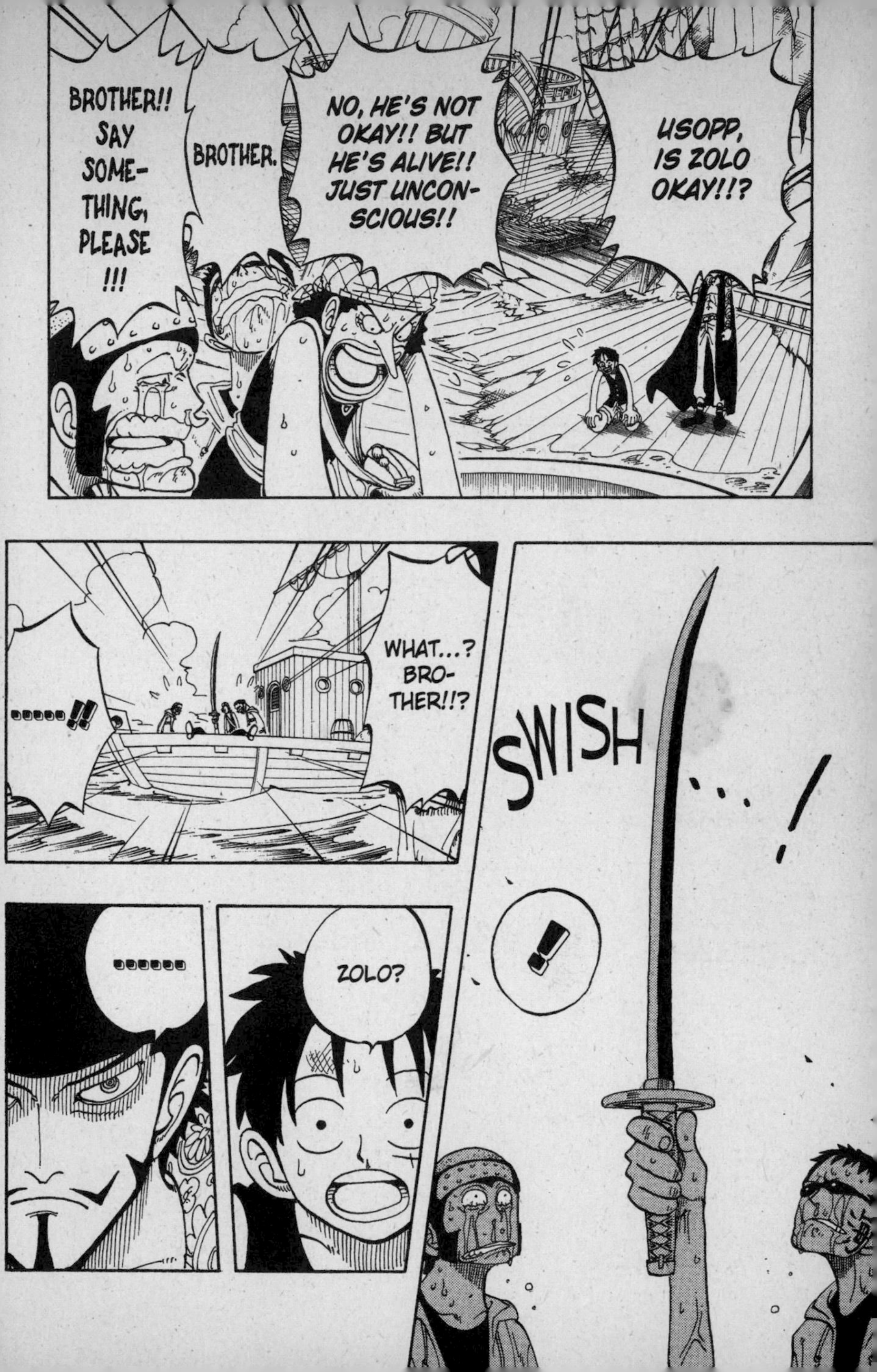

USOPP, IS ZOLO OKAY!!?
NO, HE'S NOT OKAY!! BUT HE'S ALIVE!! JUST UNCONSCIOUS!!
BROTHER.
BROTHER!! SAY SOMETHING, PLEASE!!!
WHAT...? BROTHER!!?
......!!
......
ZOLO?
SWISH
...!
!

LU-
LUFFY...?
CAN YOU... HEAR ME?
I HEAR YOU!!
......
WERE YOU WORRIED ?
PFF
HFF
IF I FAIL...
TO BECOME THE WORLD'S GREATEST SWORDS-MAN...
YOU'LL BE DISAPPOINTED, RIGHT!!?
SPUT!!
BROTHER!! SAVE YOUR BREATH!!
BROTHER!!
NEVER AGAIN!!

I WILL NEVER LOSE AGAIN !!!
FROM NOW TO THE DAY I BEAT HIM TO BECOME THE GREATEST SWORDS-MAN...
...
...I WILL NEVER...
LOSE AGAIN !!!!

READ THIS WAY

GOT A PROBLEM WITH THAT...
...
KING OF THE PIRATES !!?

HEE HEE HEE HEE !!
NOT AT ALL!!!

THEY MAKE A GOOD TEAM.

I HOPE TO ENCOUNTER YOU TWO...
... AGAIN... SOMEDAY.
FWAP....!
!

HEY, HAWK-EYE!!
DOOM

DIDN'T YOU COME HERE FOR MY HEAD?
FOR THE HEAD OF DON KRIEG, KING OF THE EASTERN BLUE!?

THAT WAS MY INTENTION.
BUT I'VE HAD ENOUGH FUN FOR NOW, SO I SHALL TAKE A NAP.

DON'T GO JUST YET, FANCY PANTS!
YOU'VE HAD YOUR FUN, BUT I'VE ONLY BEEN ON THE RECEIVING END.

D-D-DON KRIEG !!?
IF THE MAN WANTS TO GO, FOR THE LOVE OF GOD, L-LET 'IM GO!!
OZWA

BAM BAM BAM BAM
BA
NOW IT'S MY TURN TO HAVE FUN-- DIE!!!
YOU ARE IN-DEED...
...A SLOW LEARNER.
FARE-WELL.
BOOSH!!!

THROO
WHA...
WAAAAH
AARGH!!
HE...HE ESCAPED !?

LET'S DO IT !!!
RIGHT !!
WAP!!

WE'LL SAIL FOR THE GRAND LINE!!!
AND WHEN WE'VE GOT EVERYBODY TOGETHER!!
THWAP!!
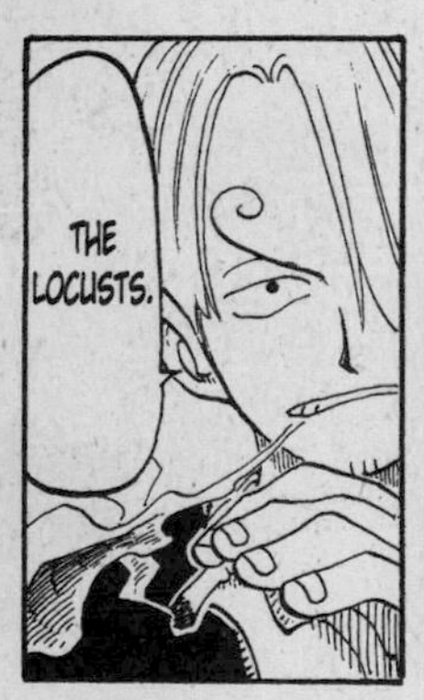
THE LOCUSTS.

HERE COME...
WOOOOO

HEY, MISTER!! IF I CHASE THOSE GUYS OFF...
CAN I STOP BEING CHORE BOY?
WOOO
WHAT? THAT'S A DEAL!

ONE PIECE **STORYBOARD PRESENTATION!!** #10

Chapter 53:
MACKEREL HEAD

BUGGY'S CREW: AFTER THE BATTLE! PART 13: "WANTED"

I WAS GOING TO SCUTTLE THAT BATTERED HULK ANYWAY...

HE JUST SAVED US THE EFFORT.

RESTAURANT

TAKE A GOOD LOOK AT THAT SHIP'S DECO-RATIONS...

READ
THIS
WAY

WITH THAT SILLY SHIP, WE CAN DOMINATE THE GRAND LINE.
IT'S BETTER THAN POSING AS A NAVY SHIP, OR WAVING A WHITE FLAG...
WE CAN APPROACH ANY SHIP WE WANT WITHOUT AROUSING SUSPICION...

...AND LAUNCH A SURPRISE ATTACK.
IT'S ALMOST FOOL-PROOF.

AYE, NOBODY'D SUSPECT THAT JOKE OF A SHIP...
TO BE FULL TO THE GILLS WITH PIRATES.
AND THESE DAYS, THE SEAS ARE ROTTEN WITH OUT-OF-WORK PIRATES.
ASSEMBLING ANOTHER FLEET SHOULD BE CHILD'S PLAY!!

B-BUT DON KRIEG! IF WE GO BACK TO THE GRAND LINE...
WE MIGHT MEET OTHERS LIKE THAT HAWK-EYE!!
BAM
BAM
BAM!!
OOGH!!!

ANY MORE COWARDS AMONG YOU!? STEP FORWARD!!
SPLASH!!
N-NO...
DO YOU REALLY THINK THAT A NORMAL MAN COULD SPLIT A GIGANTIC GALLEON WITH A SWORD!!?

HUH!? WHAT DO YOU MEAN!?
IT'S OBVIOUS!! HE HAD THE POWER OF THE DEVIL FRUIT!!

!

HE HAS EATEN OF THE LEGENDARY DEVIL FRUIT...
THE GRAND LINE'S CRAWLING WITH PEOPLE LIKE THAT!!!

WHEN HE BROKE MY SHIP, HE PROBABLY USED SOME DEVIL-FRUIT POWER!!!
ON THE GRAND LINE, THAT STRAW-HAT BRAT WILL BE JUST ANOTHER PIRATE...

BUT "RED SHOES" ZEFF...
HE SAILED THE GRAND LINE FOR A *WHOLE YEAR.*
HE MUST KNOW SOME SECRET FOR SAILING AMONG THOSE FREAKS!!

ALL RIGHT, YE SEA-WOLVES!! LET'S CAPTURE THAT FISH!!!

YARRRRR !!!!

WOW!
THEY'RE PRETTY WORKED UP!! THIS SHOULD BE FUN!!

HEY, MISTER! YOU PROMISE, RIGHT!?
I COULDN'T HOPE FOR A BETTER DEAL.
IF YOU STAYED A WHOLE YEAR, MY SHIP WOULD BE A WRECK.
WHERE'S PATTY AND CARNE?
READY AND ITCHING TO GO!
THOSE TWO ARE GREAT AT TIMES LIKE THESE!!

BUT ONLY AT TIMES LIKE THESE...GO TO THE CONTROL ROOM AND OPEN THE FINS.
HUH...YOU SURE!? WON'T THAT GIVE THE PIRATES A FOOTHOLD?
THAT'S WHAT WE WANT.

IF WE WRECK THE WHOLE RESTAURANT THE CRAP-GEEZER WILL HOWL.
WHAT WAS THAT, CRAP-KID?
I SAID YOU'D SCREAM LIKE A BABY.
TMPTMP
I'M OUTTA HERE!

VROINNNG...!!
GUM-GUM...
HERE I GO.
HAND OVER THAT SHIP, GRUB MONKEYS!!!
OOOO
SNAP!!
ROCKET!!!
VWOOOOM
AND!!
WHUP!!
HEY!! HE'S FLYING TOWARD US!!!
Fight:

GIANT SCYTHE !!!!
BASH!!
TOOF !!!!
-SPLOOOSH
GLUB
GLUB
GACK!!
WAP

HOORAY!!
GOOD JOB, CHORE BOY!!!
THE GRAND LINE'S CRAWLING WITH PEOPLE LIKE THAT, EH?
YOU UNGRATEFUL JERK...I'LL KNOCK YOU TO THE MOON!!
HA HA HA!!
SO YOU BROUGHT THE FIGHT TO US ON THE WATER, WHERE YOU CAN'T MOVE FREELY.
I KNOW THAT YOU DEVIL-FRUIT FREAKS SINK LIKE STONES IN THE SEA!
ANCHOR BOY.
YEAH, BUT I CAN STILL STRETCH!
FORWARD!!!

BOOM-DA♪ BOOM-DA♪
BARATIE NAVAL WARFARE WEAPON!! MACKEREL HEAD I !!!
ANYONE WHO DOESN'T WANNA DIE HAD BETTER SWIM FOR IT!!!
BOOM-DA-♫ BOOM-DA♪
KLANK
SKREEK SKREEK
FWAP!!
KLUNK!!
KLANG!
BOOM-DA♪ BOOM-DA♪
WHAT IS THAT?
WOW
YEAH!
COOL!!!
SKREEK SKREEK
SPLASH!!
BOOM-DA♪ BOOM-BOOM-BOOM!
TH-THE FISH'S HEAD!!!
WHAT!!!

DOOM!!

IT POPPED OFF!!?

C'MON, ROW FASTER!!

WUP WUP WUP WUP

YOU ROW FASTER!!

I'M TRYING!!

SPLASH SPLASH SPLASH SPLASH...!!

WOOOO
IT'S HERE!!!
FIRE!!
AYE-AYE!!!
BOOM BOOM!!
WAAAAAAH!!

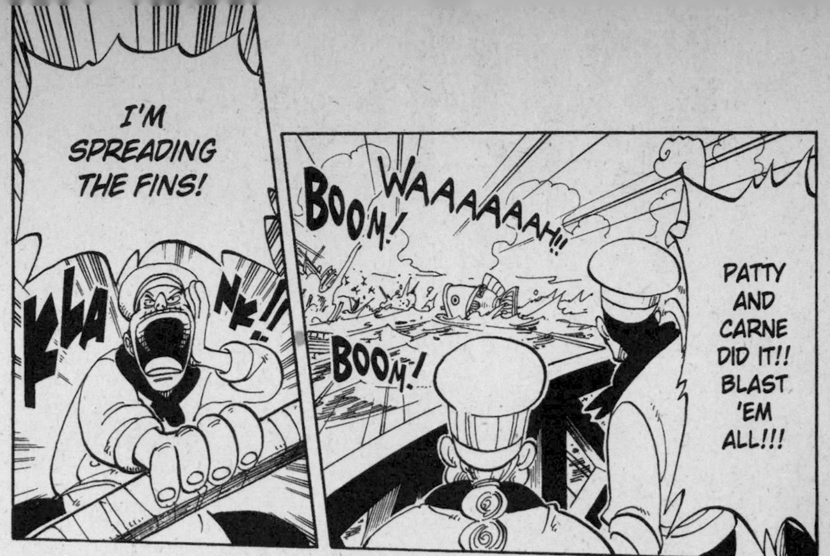
BOOM!
WAAAAAAAH!!
PATTY AND CARNE DID IT!! BLAST 'EM ALL!!!
BOOM!
I'M SPREADING THE FINS!
KLANK!!

KREEEEEEEE...
NOW WHAT ARE THEY...?
YIKES!! YIKES!! I'M SINKING!!

KROOOOM
THOOM...
NOW YOU CAN FIGHT YOUR-SELVES SILLY, PIRATES.

SPLOOSH
WHAT IS IT!!?
AAAAH!!

KLUNK!!
IT'S A DECK!!!
BOOM BOOM! WAAAAH BOOM
FROM THE OCEAN DEPTHS...

TMP...
AH...A FIGHTING DECK, TO KEEP THE RESTAURANT FROM GETTING DAMAGED.
AND AD-VANTAGEOUS FOR US, TOO, SINCE THAT SHIP WILL SOON BE OURS...
I WANT IT MORE THAN EVER, NOW!

IT'S INGENIOUS!!!
WOW

DOGON!

RESTAURANT

BARATIE

BWA HA HA HA HA!! GO GET 'EM!! SERVE 'EM UP A BIG POT OF DEFEAT!!!
WUP WUP WUP
PATTY!! EYES FORWARD!! I'M HEADING FOR KRIEG!!!
ALL RIGHT, KRIEG!! PREPARE TO DIE!!!
BOOM BOOM!
FEEL THE POWER OF THE MACKEREL HEAD I, THE PRIDE OF BARATIE!!!
!
KA-BOOM!!
PREPARE TO BE SHARK FOOD!!
WaHaHaHa!
RAARR
KLUNK!! KLUNK!!

WUP WUP WUP WUP
W- WE'RE NOT MOVING !!!
WHAT !!?
SPLAP SPLAP SPLAP

VREEN ...
I AM DON KRIEG.
RULER OF THE WORLD'S SEAS!!

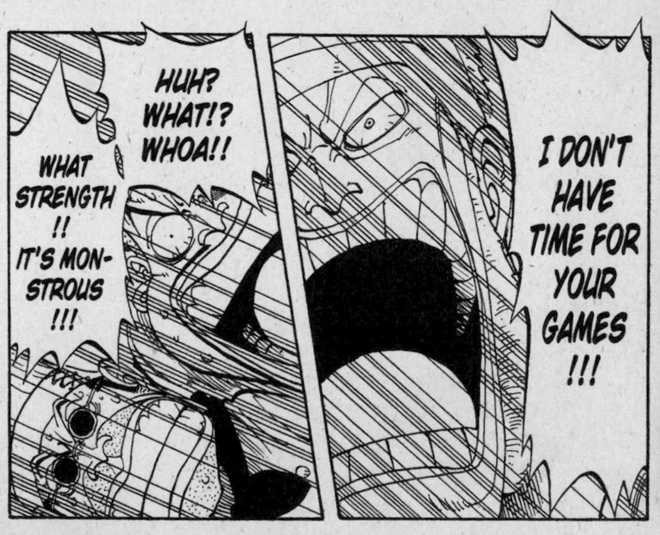
HUH? WHAT!? WHOA!!
WHAT STRENGTH !! IT'S MON-STROUS !!!
I DON'T HAVE TIME FOR YOUR GAMES !!!

G-R-R-R
HEY, THAT'S GONNA BE ME!!

THOSE TWO HAD A LOT OF HEART.
SWUP
SIGH
WAAAH!!
WE'RE GONNA HIT THE RESTAU-RANT!!
THW
!!?
SANJI!!!
WITH ONE KICK !?
AK...
HEH HEH...

AM I GAUDY?

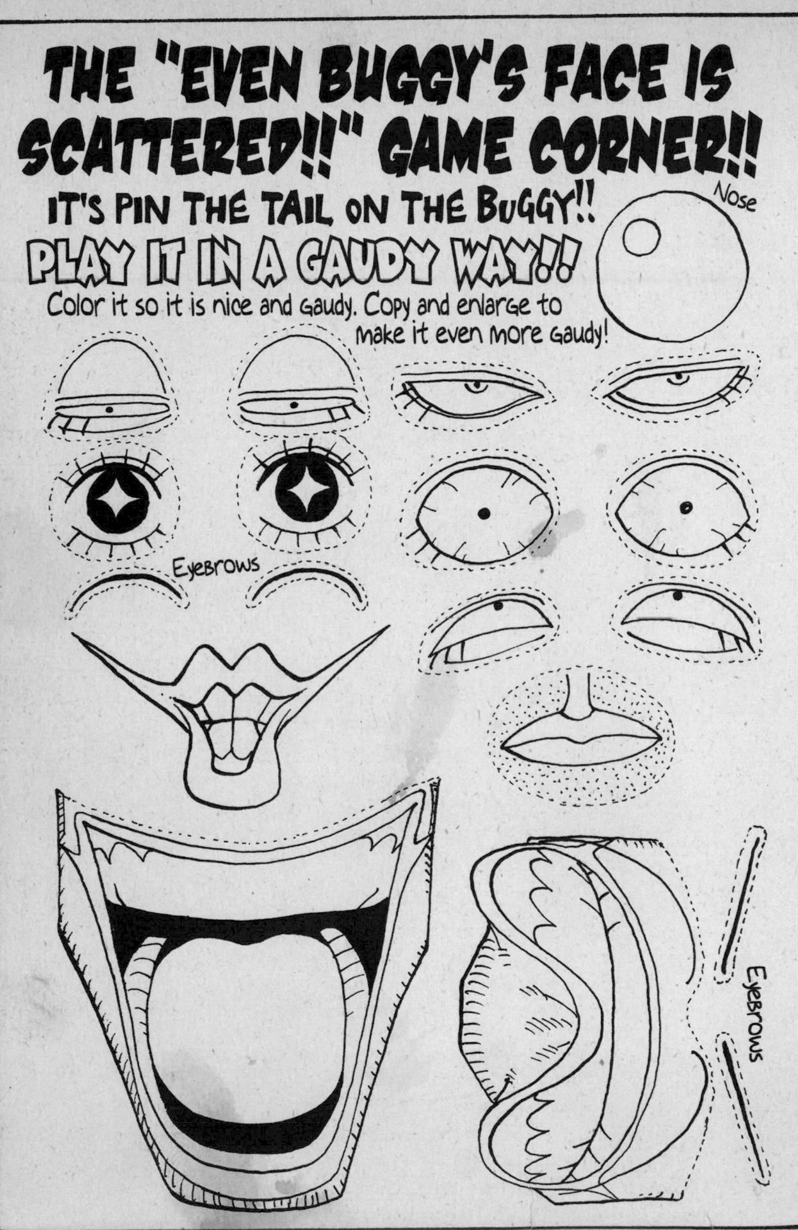
THE "EVEN BUGGY'S FACE IS SCATTERED!!" GAME CORNER!!
IT'S PIN THE TAIL ON THE BUGGY!!
PLAY IT IN A GAUDY WAY!!
Color it so it is nice and gaudy. Copy and enlarge to make it even more gaudy!
Nose
Eyebrows
Eyebrows

COMING NEXT VOLUME:

The indefatigable Don Krieg brings out his secret weapon in the form of a shiny Pearl...but that won't stop Sanji from protecting his beloved Baratie. It turns out Sanji owes the Crap-Geezer a big favor. Meanwhile, Luffy gets in the middle of things and tries his rubber powers against the dreadful Don Krieg, but it all boils down to Krieg's Pirate-at-Arms Gin, and the ill-fated favor he owes Sanji.

ON SALE NOW!

SHONEN JUMP™

THE WORLD'S MOST POPULAR MANGA

12 ISSUES FOR ONLY $29^{95}*

THAT'S 50% OFF THE NEWSSTAND PRICE!

Each issue of SHONEN JUMP contains the coolest manga available in the U.S., anime news, and info on video & card games, toys AND more!

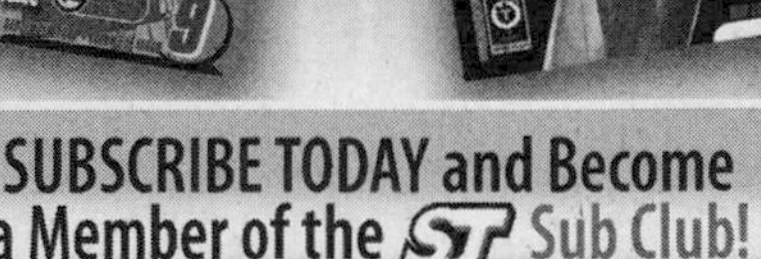

SUBSCRIBE TODAY and Become a Member of the SJ Sub Club!

- **ENJOY** 12 HUGE action-packed issues
- **SAVE** 50% OFF the cover price
- **ACCESS** exclusive areas of www.shonenjump.com
- **RECEIVE** FREE members-only gifts

Available ONLY to Subscribers!

ratings.viz.com

www.viz.com

3 EASY WAYS TO SUBSCRIBE!

1) Send in the subscription order form from this book **OR**
2) Log on to: www.shonenjump.com **OR**
3) Call 1-800-541-7919

*Canada price for 12 issues: $41.95 USD, including GST, HST, and QST. US/CAN orders only. Allow 6-8 weeks for delivery.

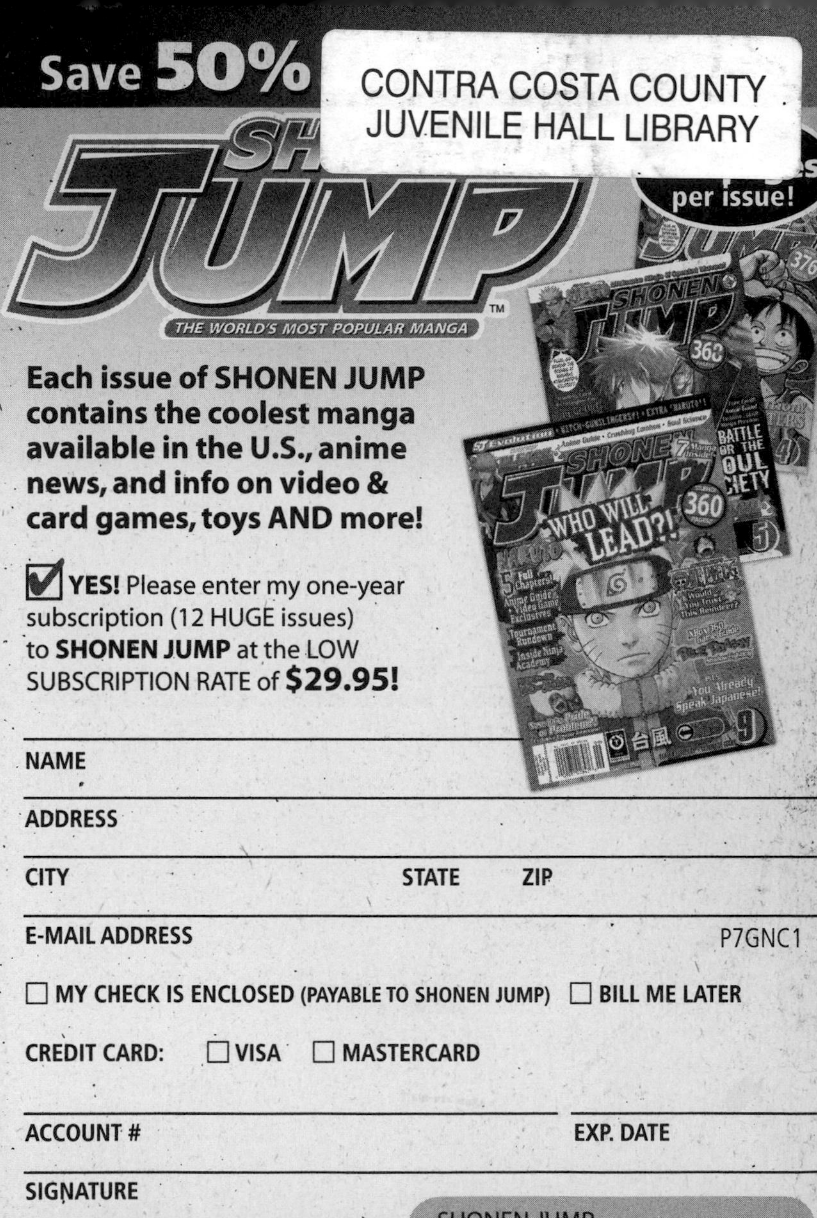

Each issue of SHONEN JUMP contains the coolest manga available in the U.S., anime news, and info on video & card games, toys AND more!

☑ **YES!** Please enter my one-year subscription (12 HUGE issues) to **SHONEN JUMP** at the LOW SUBSCRIPTION RATE of **$29.95!**

NAME

ADDRESS

CITY **STATE** **ZIP**

E-MAIL ADDRESS P7GNC1

☐ **MY CHECK IS ENCLOSED (PAYABLE TO SHONEN JUMP)** ☐ **BILL ME LATER**

CREDIT CARD: ☐ **VISA** ☐ **MASTERCARD**

ACCOUNT # **EXP. DATE**

SIGNATURE

CLIP AND MAIL TO

SHONEN JUMP
Subscriptions Service Dept.
P.O. Box 515
Mount Morris, IL 61054-0515

Make checks payable to: **SHONEN JUMP**. Canada price for 12 issues: $41.95 USD, including GST, HST and QST. US/CAN orders only. Allow 6-8 weeks for delivery.

RATED T TEEN ratings.viz.com